My Mother, My Master

Swami Pranavamritananda Puri

My Mother, My Master

Swami Pranavamritananda Puri

Mata Amritanandamayi Mission Trust
Amritapuri, Kerala, India

My Mother, My Master
By Swami Pranavamritananda Puri

Published by:
Mata Amritanandamayi Mission Trust
Amritapuri P.O., Kollam Dt.,
Kerala 690525, India
Website: www.amritapuri.org
Email: inform@amritapuri.org

First Edition, September 2012: 3,000 copies
Also available from:
Mata Amritanandamayi Center
P.O. Box 613
San Ramon, CA 94583-0613 USA
Tel: (510) 537-9417
Website: www.amma.org

Dedication

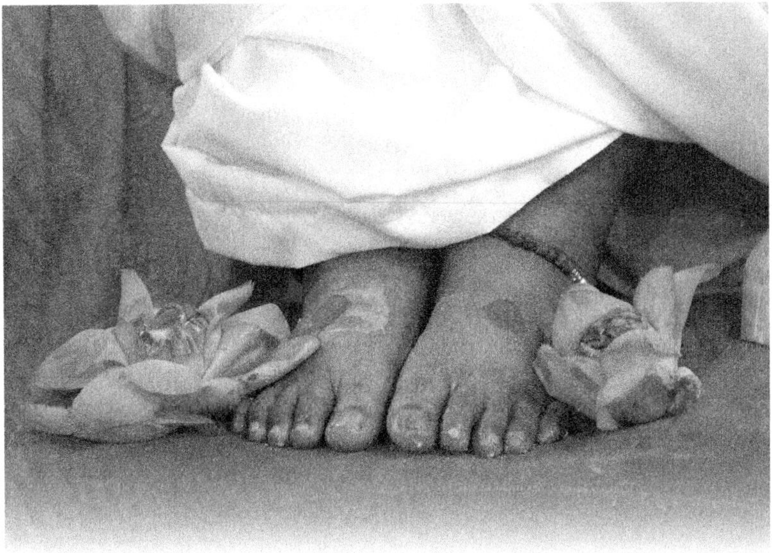

I humbly offer this book at the sacred feet of
my Mother and Master,
Śrī Mātā Amṛtānandamayī Dēvī.

Contents

Preface 10

Part 1: Awakening

1. Blessed Birth 23
2. Initial Inspirations 25
3. Baffled Bearings 29
4. Converging Courses 31
5. Master Mind 36
6. Mystic Moments 40
7. Supernal Scenes 47
8. Sweet Sensitivity 50
9. Seesawing Sentiment 53

Part 2: Analysis

10. Deep Deliberation 61
11. Kaivartakaḥ Kēśavaḥ 64
12. Dwāpara Dusk 73
13. Divine Darśan 81
14. Spiritual Sunrise 86
15. Testing Time 88
16. Selfsame Soul 95
17. Lordly Līlās 107
18. Numinous Nṛtta 112

Part 3: Approbation

19. Sacred Silence 121
20. Queenly Qualm 126
21. Broken Bond 129
22. Glorious Goddess 133
23. Fragrant Fusion 139
24. Providential Pull 145
25. Total Transformation 151
26. Sanctum Sanctorum 157
27. Ambrosial Advice 163

Part 4: Acceptance

28. Selfless Service 181
29. Sweet Spats 187
30. Primordial Pose 190
31. Extraordinary Exegete 193
32. Coherent Compassion 200
33. Real Rationalism 205
34. Dispelled Doubts 211
35. Master Musician 216
36. Midnight Melody 221

Part 5: Auspiciousness

37. Enshrined Ethos 229

38. Manifold Magnificence 234

39. Striking Similarity 239

40. Enchanting Energy 243

41. Egoless Existence 248

42. Sublime Sagacity 253

43. Masterly Mandate 263

44. Anchoritic Acuity 267

45. Sagely Subtlety 275

Glossary 287

Acknowledgments 299

Pronunciation Guide 301

Preface

There was a time when, as a college student, I found myself caught in the crossroads of material and spiritual life, the one all glitz and glamour, and the other a natural consequence of the religious and cultural grooming I enjoyed as a child and teenager. The Unseen Hand that directed me along the destined path of spirituality proved to be Amma's.

And yet, the fear of losing the material trail made me resist this Master when the opportunity of meeting Her presented itself. One day, sitting alone in a room in my aunt's house, Amma entered unannounced. Her touch had a profoundly galvanizing effect that nothing, least of all the logic and rationale I had so prided myself on, could suppress. Shocked, I fled to another room.

While trying to reckon with what had happened, questions on meditation that I had been pondering over earlier

once again surfaced. Moments later, Amma entered the room with a few devotees in tow. While speaking to them, She delved into the topic of meditation and cleared all my doubts in simple language, driving home the points with homely parables and anecdotes. I was dumbfounded.

Much later, I learned that Amma had told a few devotees, "Vēṇu is my son. He will come to Amma." She had said this even before I met Her. This, together with other events that followed then and later in my life as a *brahmacāri* (novice) and *sanyāsi* (ordained monk) in Her order, left no doubt in my mind that She is a living spiritual Master in every sense of the term.

The roots of my spiritual life were watered by my family's association with the Cheṭṭikuḷangara Bhagavatī Temple and the allied religious culture, as well as my personal devotion to Kṛṣṇa. This background helped me relate in a meaningful way to the Bhāva darśans, which cemented my personal relationship with the Divine, and which are part of the āśram's hallowed history. Amma no longer manifests the Kṛṣṇa Bhāva, and Dēvī Bhāva darśans are much rarer now than they were before, but both were a distinctive feature of the āśram's earliest phase, when I joined Amma's order as a brahmacāri, the fourth after Br. Uṇṇikṛṣṇan (now Swāmi Turīyāmṛtānanda Puri), Br. Bālagōpāl (now Swāmi Amṛtaswarūpānanda Puri) and Br.

Nīlu (now Swāmi Paramātmānanda Puri). For this reason, I have dwelled at some length on the bhāva darśans in the chapters that follow.

Many are the experiences recounted by the ever-increasing tribe of devotees about encounters with Amma's omniscience and omnipotence. Even though She discourages a fixation on mystical feats, Her ability to understand the minds of Her yearning devotees, comfort and guide them, wherever they might be, has been amply acknowledged and corroborated by Her followers all over the world.

The immortal verse from the *Bhagavad Gītā*, "*Yadā yadā hi dharmasya glānirbhavati Bhārata / abhyutthānamadharmasya tadātmānam sṛjāmyaham*" ("O Arjuna, whenever righteousness declines and unrighteousness flourishes, I incarnate (for the establishment of righteousness)") (4.7) is relevant to Amma's mission, which is nothing other than the reinstating of *dharma* (righteousness), which She continues to do, disregarding compromises to Her own physical well-being.

Recently, in an interview, a journalist asked Amma, "In Your vision, where do you see the āśram 10 years from now?"

In Her disarmingly simple way, She replied, "The work we have done so far was not pre-planned. Whenever the need arose, we formulated a course of action befitting the situation. We have been like a river, going with the flow."

Amma is both the 'flow' and 'current' of the river, its direction and velocity. Not only has She initiated an unbroken torrent of selfless service over the last few decades, Amma has done it with such unprecedented intensity and outreach as to have set a high watermark for humanitarian activities. Hailed all over the world as the 'Hugging Saint,' Her purposefulness is demonstrated by Her darśans, which stretch up to 18 hours a day.

Once, a sanyāsi known for his quick wit went with a few devotees to the venue where Amma was giving darśan. The milling crowd made the task of admitting visitors at the access points very difficult. The monk and his team were stopped at an enclosure, a volunteer asserting that the passage was meant for women only. Pat came the monk's reply: "Don't you know what Mīrā Dēvī once said when she was denied entry to an assembly of monks? She said that there was only one Man[1] and He was Kṛṣṇa. Likewise, the only *Puruṣa* here is Amma, and She is giving darśan right now!" Saying so, he quickly went past the cordon.

Amma makes Herself available to anyone who wishes to receive Her blessings. Darśan literally means 'to see.' Traditionally, a Master is only seen but not touched, but with Amma, darśan has come to mean a signature hug.

1 A play on the word 'Puruṣaḥ,' which means 'man' in Malayāḷam, and 'Supreme Self' in Sānskṛt

This unique darśan is Her concept, the awareness that all are one, inimitably translated to action. Amma's maternal hands bind the recipient in a warm embrace that thaws the coldest barriers of tradition, sex, class, creed, color and country, Her hands forming a ring of infinity that encompasses everything, including dualities and contradictions. Through that hug, Amma transmits Her pure and divine love. Our inner purity determines our receptivity to the lofty '*darśanam*' (divine or contemplative insight).

In the prevailing cultural milieu of Kēraḷa, where physical contact between men and women is highly restricted, Amma's darśan is unique and unparalleled, an expression of unconditional love in letter and spirit, like a loving mother hailing and holding her child in her arms. Once ushered into the overwhelming presence of this Master, the sway of Her gaze and sweetness of Her smile captivate everyone. Her embrace elevates the devotee to a state of exhilaration, the soulful syllables breathed into the ears quicken the spirit, the gentle peck on the cheek makes children of us all, and *prasād* (consecrated gift) becomes a tangible token of motherly love.

It is commonly thought that temple worship and listening to sermons alone constitute spirituality and are sufficient for one's spiritual elevation. Although these are definitely beneficial, they cannot take an aspirant to final liberation. Only a Guru, established in the Supreme, can.

"The Buddhas do but tell the way; it is for you to swelter at the task," said the Buddha. There was a time when Masters were signposts pointing to liberation and eternal happiness. Amma has breathed new life into the role of the Guru, traveling down the road to liberation with the seeker and negotiating perilous crossroads until the seeker reaches his destination. In keeping with Her ageless wisdom, She is able to reinterpret the old truths in new ways for seekers of Truth.

The most that even a master portraitist can hope to do is to sketch a picture of Amma, Her external lineaments, captivating features and beatific smile. No static picture can capture Her myriad, beguiling moods and the inner radiance that shines through Her. And so, with utmost humility, I have sought to complement the central thread of the narrative with philosophical reflection, accentuating the import by quotes from the scriptures and noted thinkers, both Western and Eastern. I have taken the liberty of employing the discursive mode of writing to meander down the mind's byways, which, to my mind, enriches the narrative.

Disciples and devotees have written much about Amma, waxing lyrical about Her many-sided personality. In writing this book, I have essentially traversed similar ground, and at the same time, striven to probe the philosophical underpinnings of my early experiences with Amma. Larger than life, and unparalleled in history, Amma is a living scripture whose wealth can be unearthed through exegesis, and I have tried to express my humble understanding of my Mother and Master, intuitively trying to answer the question "What makes Her tick?"

Having spent more than three decades in Amma's monastic order as a permanent resident, I am convinced that Her sphere of influence is not just confined to the field of *karma* (action). Her diminutive physical form belies a colossal metaphysical power—that is the only explanation for Her staggering indefatigability.

Fire has been a leitmotif in spiritual literature since time immemorial, and a metaphor for everything from desire to Realization. Fire reaches out to us as light, heat and sustenance. Just as anything that comes into extended contact with fire is purified of its dross, anyone who comes into protracted contact with the Guru's divine effulgence is rid of his impurities (desires).

Here is a fire of knowledge and selfless love, which sets our inner faculties aglow, burns our dross, and imparts cool and calm. The tears that flow when the heart is overwhelmed by the Guru's ineffable love kindle the light within, stoking it into brilliance. We realize then that these sacred teardrops feed the fire of devotion.

In today's world, where a sincere smile, a loving word or a compassionate look is conspicuous by its absence, Amma is a welcome exception. She has inspired many to a life of humanitarian service, and transformed countless more. Many of us who follow Amma have learned from Her the art of smiling from the heart, thus bringing about a smile on the faces of others. I have attempted to convey my experience of this cosmic phenomenon, Amma, in words and phrases that are pitiably inadequate for the purpose. This humble work, I dedicate at Her Lotus Feet. *Aum amṛtēśwaryai namaḥ.*

yā niśā sarvabhūtānām tasyām jāgarti samyamī
yasyām jāgrati bhūtāni sā niśā paśyatō munēḥ
That which is night to all beings, in that the self-controlled man wakes. That in which all beings wake, is night to the Self-seeing sage.

(Bhagavad Gītā, 2.69)

Part One
Awakening

1

Blessed Birth

The *Ṛg-Vēda*[2] opens with "*Agnimīḷē*," which means "I praise Agni (Lord of Fire)," who is seated before my very eyes, here in the form of the glorious Master, Amma. Agni (fire) symbolizes the light of spiritual knowledge leading one to Truth. Agni is nothing other than the innermost light that shines in all things, sentient and insentient, as the Self, as inner consciousness. The supreme state of pure knowledge alluded to—effulgent Awareness, proclaimed and praised by the four-fold Vēdas—is manifest, right here in our presence for us to behold, in the form of Amma.

2 'Ṛg' is derived from the root 'Ṛc,' meaning 'to praise.' The Ṛg-Vēda is made up of hymns in praise of the Divine. The great sages of yore are said to have perceived the eternal truths, and bequeathed to posterity their apprehensions of the numinous. These sagely revelations came to be known as Vēdas, of which there are four: Ṛg, Yajus, Sāma and Atharva.

Having come face to face with Amma's many-splendored dimension over the last few decades, there is no doubt in my mind that Amma in Her gross and subtle forms represents pure knowledge, bearing out the eternal Ṛg-Vēdic mantra[3] starting with "*Agnimīḷē purōhitam.*" She is indeed seated right before us, radiant with love and compassion.

"*Hanta Bhāgyam Janānām*" ("O, the great good fortune of the people") sang Melpattūr Nārāyaṇa Bhaṭṭatiri.[4] He could well have been expressing *our* singularly good fortune, since we have been blessed to be born and to live when the Supreme Goddess Herself has descended into our midst in human form.

We are all earnestly committed to worldly activities. Do we have the same dedication to discovering our Self? More often than not, the answer is no. We have scaled the heights of many mountains, but have remained woefully ignorant of our own Self and its native glory. Amma has reiterated time and again that the goal of life is Self-realization. It follows that all our endeavors should be directed to this lofty objective.

---

3 A sound, syllable, word or words of spiritual content. According to Vēdic commentators, mantras are revelations of ṛṣis arising from deep contemplation.

4 A great poet and Sānskṛt scholar who authored the immortal literary work, Nārāyaṇīyam, a synoptic rendition of the Bhāgavata Purāṇa, extolling the life and times of all the 10 incarnations of Lord Viṣṇu, especially Lord Kṛṣṇa.

It is ironic that though the key to spiritual liberation is within easy reach, we choose to remain in the prison-house of material desires. Amma, the divine incarnation, is waiting with outstretched arms to elevate us from the ruts of ignorance to spiritual heights. Let us no longer resist this fresh and fragrant air of spiritual understanding that Amma is infusing into our lives.

2

Initial Inspirations

I had an inborn leaning towards spirituality, and nurtured a desire to tread the path. The life and works of great Masters like Ādi Śankara[5] and Śrī Rāmakṛṣṇa Paramahamsa influenced me profoundly, urging me to rise from the mundane to the sublime.

The Malayāḷam biopic on Jagadguru Ādi Śankara made such a deep impression on my mind, so roused my latent desire to renounce the world, that I saw the movie at least a

5 *Also known as Ādi Śankarācārya*

dozen times. *'Jagadguru Ādi Śankaran'* cogently conveys the subtle import of spiritual practices as well as interpretations of Vēdic philosophy. This heady concoction was, for me, a rare treat, and for society, food for profound thought. I was so intoxicated by the movie that I would have continued watching it, but the local theater stopped screening it after some time. The film also whetted my appetite for the knowledge of Sānskṛt.

I started smearing holy ash on my forehead, and stopped singing all but devotional songs, especially *'Bhaja-gōvindam,'* a hymn composed by Ādi Śankara. My passion for music was well known in college. When my college mates asked me to sing popular film songs of the day, I would oblige them only with songs from the movie on Ādi Śankara or other devotional numbers.

In the meantime, practicing meditation became part of my daily routine, its subtle effect making me less inclined to speak, and compelling me more or less to a vow of silence. My friends, noticing the marked change in my demeanor, inquired into the reasons for it. I told them that life was not meant exclusively for sensual gratification, alluding to the lofty target on which I had set my sights.

Doubts began to rise in my mind the more I thought about this pursuit. I sought clarification of these doubts from various sources, including sanyāsis, but none could resolve them. As if in response to my fervid yearning, a cooling breeze bearing a divine fragrance wafted my way one day at the end of 1979.

I was about 20 years old when this seemingly fortuitous meeting took place. In hindsight, it is clear that Amma's advent into my life was preordained. I later learned that She had, in fact, prophesied that I would come to Her, i.e. become Her disciple, sooner rather than later. My birth brother, Bālagōpāl (now Swāmi Amṛtaswarūpānanda Puri), who had already become a disciple by then, was the butt of some innocuous jokes by Amma, who said that the prospect of my joining Her had given him sleepless nights spent worrying that I might snatch away Amma's love and concern for him!

3

Baffled Bearings

One day, Saraswatiyamma, my *Vallyammachi*,[6] sent an acquaintance to fetch me from college. It seemed Amma had arrived at my aunt's house with a group of devotees, and was due to spend the day there with my aunt, like She used to once in a while. I did not go, even though the messenger took pains to stress my aunt's request. When he left, disappointment was writ large on his face.

I was going through a very disturbing phase, my mind torn between the meretricious attractions of material life and the radiant glow on the spiritual horizon beckoning me. The prospect of abandoning college studies was as disquieting as the thought of forgoing the fulfillment I could find in

6 *Mother's elder sister, otherwise referred to as aunt. After my mother's early demise, my elder brother Bālagōpāl stayed with our father at Harippāṭ, while I stayed in Māvēlikkara with my Vallyammachi, her husband and her mother (my grandmother). When I finished 10th grade, I moved to Harippāṭ. From there, I would commute to Bishop Moore College at Māvēlikkara for my Bachelor's degree. After my father's second marriage, I gained two sisters and a brother. Our mother, whom we lovingly called 'Harippāṭ-amma,' showered her undivided care and attention on all five of us. In later years, both she and my father became ardent devotees of Amma.*

spirituality. The dividends of a successful education seemed to outweigh the harvest that spiritual striving would yield. My forays into music and singing had brought me a few laurels during my college days, giving a boost to my young ego. Instinctively, I felt that I would have to give up college life if I were to meet Amma, and this led to my reluctance to meet Her. As it transpired, my conjecture proved right since I did leave college but only to continue my studies under Amma's tutelage.

Once I came into Her fold, I became indifferent to academic life. But Amma did not indulge in my disinclination. She firmly said, "You should sit for the examinations. Don't worry. Amma will take care of everything."

Unable to disobey Her, I appeared for the B.Sc. Zoology final examinations. Arriving barefoot at the examination hall, clad in a *dhōti* and a faded, crumpled *kurta*,[7] my forehead and upper limbs heavily smeared with holy ash, I must have looked a sight to my college-mates, who humorously referred to me as Bhasmāsura.[8] My mind was as blank as a clean slate, and I answered just a few questions. I spent the rest of the time writing devotional songs and prayers

7 Dhōti – garment worn by men, consisting of a cloth tied around the waist and extending to the ankles; kurta – loose (and sometimes, collarless) shirt.
8 A Purāṇic character; in this context, a jocular reference to someone smeared with ash.

for the Zoology exams, a sure way of failing, but when the results came, I found that I had passed! Perhaps, the examiners were God believers who had been moved by the unexpected display of devotion. Also, the external examiners had helped me dissect the biological test specimens during the laboratory examinations. I had no explanation for all these. I could only ascribe my passing of the examinations to the Master's omnipotence and assurances.

4

Converging Courses

My studies at the Bishop Moore College at Māvēlikkara, my friends there and campus life in general were all dear to me, as were my family life, the home environment, weekends and local festivals. These were the warp and woof of my life's fabric, and the thought of tearing myself away from them was unimaginably painful.

Whenever I was in college, my mind would be drawn irresistibly towards the collegiate life. The hero worship I enjoyed because of my singing was so flattering that I began seriously considering giving up spiritual life. But away from college, my thoughts would wander toward the spiritual path, and I would intuit the fulfillment I stood to enjoy there. Reflections on life's loftier purposes would repeatedly rouse my mind, becoming a soft sell for the quest of God. The result was an on-going tug of war between these divergent attractions.

At around this time, in December 1979, I went for the annual study tour with my zoology classmates. A college excursion typically involves traveling, studying, working, eating and staying together. This trip added to my sense of restlessness, and I wondered if the conflict in my mind had not become worse.

After the trip, I set out to catch a bus to my house in Harippāṭ. Lost in thought, I started walking from the college to the bus-stand near the house of my aunt. She had temporarily shifted to this rented house from the original *taravāṭ*[9] at Māvēlikkara some time earlier. The joint family system of living had become irksome to her, impelling her to move to a new place. However, before long, she moved back to join her mother at the taravāṭ. This change of heart can be attributed to Amma's association with the family.

Walking up to the road junction, the statue of the meditating Buddha (known locally as 'Putracchan'), which was near

9 *The household of the main family in a matriarchal system.*

the bus-stand, came into view. Then everything happened in a flash. Some unseen force prevailed on me to go to my aunt's house nearby. I had wanted to go to Harippāṭ, but here I was, as if possessed by some strange conviction, walking towards my aunt's place. The conflict that had been tormenting my mind until that moment mysteriously vanished.

The Kēraḷa coast and the thin belt of the hinterland in the Western Ghats—which mostly hemmed its limits, separating it from the neighboring states—were, historically, a flourishing landmass. Its general affluence and numerous traditional art forms drew several religious, trading and warring communities, which settled here eventually. It is believed that the land is part of a large tract reclaimed from the sea. A group of *Brāhmins* (priest community) was the first settlers here. The locals were the indigenous tribes residing in the forests of the Western Ghats. The Jains, Buddhists, Jews, Christians and Muslims migrated to this region in later years.

Very few Buddhist relics survived the changes wrought by the passage of time, the black granite Buddha in meditative form near my aunt's house being an exception. One of the outcomes of the influx of diverse religious, trading and warring peoples from across the borders was the rise of a

dominant martial clan, which led to a period of combat and skirmishes. My aunt's rented house belonged to this warrior clan. Changes, especially after India's independence in 1947, altered the status quo, and many such palatial homes passed hands.

The statue of Putracchan was a shrine visited regularly by the devout. That day, it appeared to me a trifle more beatific than usual, as if able to guess the reason for the change in my schedule. "Just as a candle cannot burn without fire, man cannot live without a spiritual life"—the Buddha's words appeared to reflect Putracchan's mood aptly.

The prevalent belief, associated with a popular legend, is that offering coconuts to Putracchan would bring rains to the area. The occupation of people in Māvēlikkara being primarily agriculture, there was a high dependency on seasonal rains falling in time; a delay of even a week would often result in considerable losses to the average farmer. The faith in Putracchan's power to bring rains was born of the experiences of generations. This important religious and cultural landmark for both locals and the visiting crowd from far and near is presently a heritage site under the department of archaeology.

Later, I learned that Amma had gone to my aunt's rented house, and was staying there that day. Such was Her unseen but potent influence that She had literally swayed the course of my life. I believe that the dominant presence of Amma nearby, that of Lord Kṛṣṇa in the renowned Kṛṣṇaswāmi temple in the neighborhood, as well as the awe-inspiring influence of the meditating Buddha close to where I was standing had converged to reshape my destiny, a triangle of influences laying the foundation for the change in my life. This divine trinity united to change my resolve to go to Harippāṭ, prevailing on me to drop in on my aunt's house instead that day.

Never would I have guessed that the change in my plan was going to be such a momentous one, with Amma changing the course of my life forever. It revealed all the signs of a premeditated plan, executed by the cosmic hand!

5

Master Mind

Instead of going to Harippāṭ, I found myself at my aunt's house, which had several rooms connected by narrow passages. As I opened the gate, I saw a young woman standing in front of the raised portico, talking to a few people standing near Her. I saw Her glancing at me as I came in through the gate. She was dressed in white, Her head covered with the end of Her sāri, as if by a veil. There was a small group assembled there.

At first sight, She appeared to be a Muslim lady. But seeing the vermilion mark on Her forehead and a nose-ring, I decided otherwise, and marched past Her into the house. I continued to wonder who this woman could be and what She could possibly be doing in my aunt's house. Taking a second look at the small gathering, I recognized some of them, including my aunt and brother, Bālagōpāl, as devotees of Amma. It then became clear to me that the lady in white was none other than Amma Herself.

Amma even now vividly recalls that scene: the dress and hairstyle I sported then—an orange kurta with embroidered neckline paired with a pair of stylish black bell-bottomed pants, and a thick mop of hair—as well as a bag slung over my shoulders, to quote Amma's own words. That is Amma for you, remembering the smallest detail and reminding me

of what even I had forgotten about myself. We may forget Amma, but She never forgets us! Is this not the true image of the indulgent, loving Mother?

ൟ ൟ ൟ

Unique are the ways in which the Lord or Masters meet their close devotees or disciples. A tale from *Hālasyamāhātmyam,*[10] depicting Lord Śiva's love and compassion for His devotees illustrates one such novel way.

Once, when the king of the renowned Pāṇḍya empire arrived for his regular morning prayers at the famous Mīnākṣī temple, Lord Śiva appeared on the scene in the guise of an ascetic, just outside the sanctum sanctorum. When He blocked the path of the king, the royal guards ordered Him to move away, but the ascetic refused. The king demanded, "Who are you?"

"I am an ascetic of great occult powers," replied the ascetic. "I am subservient to none, and the Lord of all. I am omnipotent!"

At this point, a farmer brought a sugarcane and offered it to the king. The outer skin of the sugarcane, which was

10 Compilation of 64 tales centered around Lord Sundarēśwara (an epithet of Lord Śiva) of Madurai.

of incredibly huge length and girth, sported a captivating blend of natural hues. Determined to belittle the ascetic, the king asked Him to command the huge sculpture of the elephant in front of the shrine to eat the sugarcane out of his hand. The mystic immediately ordered the stone elephant to do so, whereupon the latter momentarily came to life, snatched the sugarcane from the king's hand and ate the sugarcane. The king's egoistic refusal to concede the ascetic's power buckled, because he realized then that the sage was none other than Lord Śiva Himself! He begged the Lord for forgiveness. The Lord blessed the king, saying that He was ever eager to meet His devotees, in particular the devout and just ruler who had always been very dear to Him.

I had heard much about Amma and how Her spiritual magnetism had captured the hearts of many. My rational mind was not willing to accept hearsay evidence of Amma's charisma; I wanted nothing less than personal experience of Her spiritual power. I kept wondering how this young woman in white could possibly be a guide in spiritual matters. Unable to reconcile the dichotomy between Her youth and the purported wisdom that belied Her age, I walked past the gathering into one of the rooms deep inside the house.

My anxiety about how Amma's spiritual charisma would induce me to give up my studies and renounce worldly life began to tell on me. My immediate instinct was to escape! I settled down on a bed, thinking hard about how to dodge the gathering. As I was figuring out the best way to flee without being seen, Amma suddenly entered the room, just as I was about to take off. How had She tracked me through the labyrinth of rooms to my lair? It would not have been easy for anyone, let alone a newcomer!

6

Mystic Moments

Taking a seat next to me on the bed, Amma grabbed my arm, shaking me out of my thoughts. Her timing could not have been more perfect; a moment later, and I would have plunged headlong into the quagmire of worldly life. As I look back, the whole episode strikes me as providential. Amma knew that the time was ripe to lead me to the path for which I was destined. She even had the satisfied look of a hunter who had managed to ensnare the prey in the nick of time!

Amma's touch sent a shock wave through my body, galvanizing every atom and cell. It was a spiritual experience of seismic proportions. Even today, the memory of those moments gives me goose-bumps. I recall a line from my grandmother's prayer, "*Kaṇṇil kāṇāy varēṇam rahasi mama kināvilenkilum Pankajākṣā!*" an invocation to Lord Kṛṣṇa, meaning, "O Lotus-eyed One, do grant me Your divine vision secretly, at least in my dreams." As a child, I used to intone this prayer with yearning, inducing a kind of 'Daffodils experience'—"They flash upon that inward eye / Which is the bliss of solitude" (William Wordsworth).

Though my fervent worship of Lord Kṛṣṇa during my childhood had given me the fleeting awareness of the divine presence on several occasions and in numerous ways, there was nothing like this moment, when the world around me seemed to vanish, and I experienced something elevating and unworldly, which I had never encountered before. It defies description. Was it the result of my deep yearning for a vision of the Divine, or was it an induction to the spiritual path?

Recovering from the first impact of Amma's divine touch, I heard Amma saying, "Son, Amma has been waiting for you." She added, "Aren't you a great singer? Amma wants to hear you sing."

Amma then introduced me to Her mother, Damayanti-*amma*, and the group of devotees who had come with Her as "Vēṇu-*mōn,*[11] a fine singer and younger brother of Bālu-mōn." Amma's endearing nature and the intimacy She showed as She took me by hand to introduce me to others disarmed me. The easy familiarity with which Amma held

11 *'Amma'—mother; 'mōn'—son.*

my arm seemed to suggest that She knew me very well. On a later occasion, I did ask Amma how She could be so informal with me then, considering that I was a virtual stranger. Her reply was deeply affecting: "Son, if you want to know me, you need to know yourself in the first place. I have always known you, because I know myself."

A beautiful verse from *'Amṛtadhāra,'* featuring Amma's divine outpourings, proclaims:

> *Ennile ñānāṇu nīyum, pinne ninnile nīyaṇu ñānum*
> The 'I' in me is 'You,' and the 'You' in you is 'I.'

Again, a thought-provoking avowal of *'Dēvī Bhāgavatam'* that comes to mind is,

> *Sarvam khalvidamēvāham*
> *Nānyadasti sanātanam*
> All this is 'I' alone. There is no 'other' eternal principle.

Like a spark that attempts to light a damp piece of firewood but fails to do so, my elation did not last, because the analytical nature of the mind tends to write off these experiences as mere fancies. Reverting to the level of an unemotional observer, I found myself consciously avoiding being taken in by the numinous experiences that defied explanation.

Soon after, I quietly moved away into another room that had a couple of wooden beds. Several thoughts were racing through my mind as I lay half-reclining on one of the beds. These thoughts gradually settled on my doubts pertaining to meditation, which had persisted despite efforts to clarify them with erudite scholars and a few venerable monks. I had never received a satisfactory explanation from any one of them.

I toyed with the idea of putting the questions I had mentally formulated to Amma should an opportunity arise. But the nagging thought of whether this young woman would be able to deal authoritatively with a subject like meditation and provide answers to my specific questions troubled my mind. With the brain held on leash, as it were, by such reflections, I dozed off. Waking up, I found Amma seated on the adjacent bed.

I was conscious of Amma's looking at me, and when I stole a glance, She would look away, pretending that She had not been watching me at all! This repeated itself a few times, and then Amma mercifully decided to end my misery. Years later, referring to this incident, Amma revealed, "I was gauging you and the nature of the random thoughts occupying your mind!"

The small group of devotees who had been with Amma arrived and sat around Her. What She did next became indelibly etched in my mind. Without any suggestion from anyone assembled there, Amma started talking to them about meditation. If this did not stump me enough, more was to follow. She dealt with the topic according to the questions I had formulated earlier. Comprehensively, and yet in simple terms, Amma discussed the issues to clear my doubts. Her words brought home the understanding that meditation is essentially the effort to become familiar with the mind, and that the purpose of meditation is Self-unfoldment. Meditation makes the mind expansive. Through meditation, a person's latent potential and hidden capacities can be awakened.

As the Buddha said, "There is nothing so disobedient as an undisciplined mind, and there is nothing so obedient as a disciplined mind," focusing on the central character of meditation and the realization of the objective.

Apart from being the very source of experience, Amma has a unique and interesting way of explaining the most complicated and subtle subjects with analogies and anecdotes laced with simple humor. At the end of the short discourse, Amma left the room, leaving me in awe of Her omniscience.

If we cannot accept the glory of elevated souls, it is because of our ego. Thinking that others cannot do what we cannot do makes us dismiss such phenomena as illogical or superstitious.

Like the dew that disappears at the first rays of the morning sun, doubts melted away, enabling me to realize that

Amma had the traits of a great Master. Her talk was so simple and soulful that not only did She address my original queries, but also delved into the finer aspects of the topic to provide a broader perspective. Her wisdom—evident from Her talk on the subject of meditation with specific focus on doubts lingering in my mind—had been revealed to clear my doubts.

Despite being mesmerized by Amma's seemingly palpable power to read and understand the thoughts of others and offer coherent answers couched in plain language dotted with similes and simple tales, I found myself reverting to my original viewpoint of including the experience as another odd instance of human capability.

The Upaniṣads[12] encourage healthy skepticism. A seeker of Truth must have both inquisitiveness, where doubt can have free play, and the openness of mind to accept the truth. I often wonder if this attitude had not helped to strengthen the foundation of my spiritual life under Amma's guidance. The mind is brought under control by constant observation and restraint. Transcendence in life is possible only through analysis.

12 The portions of the Vēdas dealing with Self-knowledge.

7

Supernal Scenes

As the morning progressed, I noticed in Amma a range of moods—now crying loudly, calling out "*Ammā! Ammā!*"; laughing with abandon at times; playfully interacting with everyone, now and then; and, at intervals, skipping about like a child amidst all. The mind can understand empirical realities, but who can fathom the super-sensual experiences of great souls? It is not an exaggeration at all to say that Amma is a wonder of wonders.

Amma all of a sudden sat cross-legged, and went into a trance lasting about three hours, a model of perfect tranquility, resembling a carved stone idol, body still and eyes half-open, revealing only the white part of the eye balls, and a couple of tear drops resting unmoving on the cheeks. This scene evoked memories of the meditative pose of Śrī Śankara in the movie I had seen a dozen times.

I noticed a likeness with the meditating pose of the Buddha I saw that morning, its dark hue similar to Amma's complexion. An inspiring thought arose, suggesting a comparison of the splendid duskiness of Amma to that of my *iṣṭa dēvata* (beloved deity) Kṛṣṇa.

Amma came out of the trance and started interacting with devotees, but again showed signs of retreating to Her deep contemplation. It was a rare sight to see the young lady who was hailed locally as a spiritual Guru act as if possessed by strong, unbridled emotions. Does Self-realization manifest itself as 'enchanted' or 'charmed' behavior, as outwardly striking body language? This exalted state is described by an aphorism from the *Nārada Bhakti Sūtras* (Sage Nārada's aphorisms on devotion)—"*Yajñātvā mattō bhavati…*" ("knowing which one becomes intoxicated") (6). It has been said about Śrī Rāmakṛṣṇa that his very life was a demonstration of such inebriated states. In a way, God-realization is, in effect, a most auspicious relocation (from body to soul) and promotion (attainment of bliss).

I once asked, "Amma, what is the experience of *samādhi?*"[13]

Amma said, "Son, nothing can be said about it since in that state (if it can be termed so), the seeker ceases to exist to register any experience. Such a condition is one that transcends all known situations." She added, "What you are seeing is a small projection of a world but I have seen millions of them. They appear merely as water bubbles to me!"

The Master knows the means and the end, having traversed the path to reach the goal. Thus, it is the Guru who

13 Absorption in transcendental reality

has to provide the direction, not the disciple, who, left on his own, knows neither the path nor the goal. A disciple who tries to choose his own path on his own initiative misses the goal and arrives somewhere else. There is so much emphasis in the world these days on 'doing something.' But in this sphere, just doing something without a Guru's guidance may take us somewhere, but not to the definite goal!

With my mind seeking to find further similarities, I recalled that the biographical events I had read of Śrī Rāmakṛṣṇa Paramahamsa had mentioned the Master exhibiting such unusual moods, reflecting the waves of inner joy. There was something extraordinary about the reflective, insightful eyes of this Master seen in the popular portrait, which brought tears to my eyes when I first saw it. Impressions from the movie on Ādi Śankara, bringing out the saint's multi-faceted nature, led me to a strong conviction on the uniqueness of each of these Self-realized Masters.

In later years, I have seen Amma conversing endearingly with plants, trees and the sea. On occasion, She would scoop sand with Her cupped palms, raising it over Her head to sprinkle it all around, a childlike amusement writ all over the face. Through such deeds, Amma seemed to be asking, "Is there anything apart from myself?" The glory of this non-dualistic vision, '*ekatva darśanam*,' has been extolled in all the Upaniṣads.

It had been a rare and eventful morning for me at my aunt's house, opening up many new vistas of life. The cup was seemingly full, yet I was looking forward to more. The reasoning mind was secretly vying to gather more proof of the mystical ways of this young woman with uncommon powers.

8

Sweet Sensitivity

It was noon. Amma started serving prasādam, taking a handful each time, and feeding it directly into the mouth of the devotees. It was then that She noticed a dog afflicted with rashes and open, foul-smelling sores, standing at the far end of the sprawling compound of the house. The personification of compassion, Amma rolled one huge ball of food in Her palm and walked towards the dog. When She came close, She put the food directly into the dog's mouth, and then surprised everyone by licking Her own palm clean of the remaining food particles.

A similar instance is recounted about Nāmdēv, a great devotee. Once, when he had sat down for his routine meal of *Dāl Roṭi*[14] with a dash of ghee (clarified butter) to go with it, all of a sudden, a dog appeared and, snatching a roṭi, ran away. Nāmdēv got up hurriedly and, grabbing the small container holding the ghee, ran after the dog, hailing it, "O Lord! How will you eat the dry roṭi all by itself? Please take this ghee with it!"

14 A meal consisting of unleavened bread made of wheat flour, and curry made of gram.

Nāmdēv, who saw God in everything, including the dog, ran after Him. The sweetness with which he addressed the canine, and the compassion behind his action reveal the sensitivity of evolved souls, who see creation as an extension of themselves.

Mahātmas (great souls) teach the world through their actions, which are verily divine. The way in which Masters like Amma view things is different from the way ordinary mortals do. William Blake wrote:

> This life's five windows of the soul
> Distorts the heavens from pole to pole,
> And leads you to believe a lie
> When you see with, not thro', the eye.

Although Amma's vision is cosmic, being able to relate to the created objects of this world as part of Herself, She has assumed the role of the understanding mother in Her day-to-day interactions with devotees and admirers.

9

Seesawing Sentiment

The day eventfully rolled on, with the resplendent Sun God, reveling in the ongoing *līlā* (divine acts) of this great Master, reluctantly arcing down the celestial path to the horizon and beneath. At dusk, the devotees gathered around Amma for bhajans. I participated, singing along with the devotees and playing the *dhōlak* (percussion instrument) as accompaniment for a couple of bhajans. The singing was quite inspiring, Amma steering the flow with effortless ease, taking minds to the depths of devotion.

I stayed at my aunt's place that night, and while preparing to leave for Harippāṭ early the next morning, my aunt asked me to inform Amma and take Her blessings before leaving. Not feeling too enthusiastic about this piece of advice, yet reluctant to ignore her instructions, given my recent experience of Amma's incomprehensible spiritual powers, I approached Amma and found Her in a mood that defied expression. She was in some kind of trance, and devotees usually avoid bothering Her during such occasions. The air of gravitas around Her was in contrast to what I had observed the day before. Not sure how to greet Amma and what to say, I stood there dithering. Showing perfect awareness of my discomfiture, Amma spoke tranquilly, "Son, are you leaving?"

In reply, I bent forward and touched the ground short of Amma's feet, indicating my plan to go back to Harippāṭ. Despite the spiritual awakening She had triggered the day before, I found myself reluctant to fall at Amma's feet. The Master's omniscience was discernible in Her spontaneous response. Instead of giving me a hug, Amma merely planted a kiss on my hand as I prepared to get up after the bow. The thoughts and actions of those who think they are clever are easily perceived by those endowed with greater wisdom.

I walked to the bus-stand and waited for the bus that would take me to Harippāṭ. When it finally came, I got in, finding an available seat next to an open window.

I was in a strange mood. My thought waves were too loud and tumultuous for me to contain; it was as if all that inner roiling had snuffed out the light of reasoning. Two categories of thoughts were pitting themselves against each other: whether I should continue in the sea of studies, career and whatever else followed; or whether I should ply my oars against that current and propel my way to Amma. The second offered a more appealing prospect, given the fresh evidence of a spiritual Master's hallmarks in Amma, gathered from personal observation and experience. The traits of an '*Avadhūtā*'[15] were apparent in Her conduct, most clearly when She had walked to the afflicted, foul-smelling dog and fed it, afterwards licking the remains of the food off Her palm. Amma had also revealed Her omniscience when She read my mind and resolved my doubts about meditation, thus placing Her well above the venerable monks I had consulted.

An unrelenting seesaw battle prevented my mind from settling down to a conclusion. Nagging thoughts about secular life threatened to arrest my flight into the spiritual skies on the wings of Amma's guidance, what with the voluptuous allure of worldly attractions seducing me into submission! Goading my mind to capitulation was the misplaced logic about whether a young woman like Amma, who had not received much formal education, could bestow on me the *summum bonum* of spiritual life, and if so, how!

Recollections of Śrī Rāmakṛṣṇa Paramahamsa's demeanor while in trance, which I had gathered from a portrait, surfaced insistently, as if urging me to cognize the similarity to Amma's behavior that morning; it had also matched the incidents in Ācārya Śankara's life, which I had learned about from the biopic, congruencies I found reassuring.

15 A liberated being who transcends social norms.

And yet, this recognition would be thrown off balance by an equally persuasive but contradicting thought, such as, "The instances of Rāmakṛṣṇa and Ādi Śankara are from a bygone era; can it happen now and can this young woman lead the way like those great Masters did?"

Reality does not change either because of our faith or lack of it. Stricken by 'analysis paralysis,' I hardly realized that an hour-and-a-half had passed. I had reached my destination, although I had not arrived at any decision. Anxieties over leaving college life and severing family ties were making me brood continuously on the nature of spiritual life. "The mind is its own place and in itself, can make a Heaven of Hell, a Hell of Heaven," wrote John Milton. Fortunately, the end of the bus ride saw the scales tipping in favor of seeking deliverance from mundane existence.

asamśayam mahābāhō manō durnigraham calam
abhyāsēna tu kauntēya vairāgyēṇa ca gṛhyatē

O mighty-armed son of Kunti, it is undoubtedly very difficult to curb the restless mind, but through constant practice and detachment, the mind can be brought under control.

(Bhagavad Gītā, 6.35)

Part Two

Analysis

10

Deep Deliberation

Life often throws up situations that test one's skills in decision-making. Logic and rationale, however sound, are not helpful when the mind is not trained in dispassionate analysis. The story of Cirakārī—told in the dialogue between Bhīṣma and Yudhiṣṭhira after the Mahābhārata war—is a parable on the wisdom of practical deliberation.

A wise, young ascetic finds himself in a tricky situation when his father, suspecting his wife's fidelity, tells him to kill his mother, and then angrily goes to the forest. The son, true to his name Cirakārī ('One who deliberates thoroughly before deciding'), always takes his time to analyze the pros and cons of any issue before arriving at any conclusion, and then acts only after due contemplation. Here, he was caught in the crosscurrents of allegiances: memories of his mother's selfless love competing against the deference he owed his father. The bond to his mother, more enduring than the severed umbilical cord, was as affecting as the implicit obedience he owed his father, who had always been a dutiful parent and preceptor.

Reeling under great stress, Cirakārī continued to mull for days on end over the options available to him, ultimately deciding to abide by the command of his father. He set about carrying out the task. He procured a sharp sword, which he spent endless hours honing and filing, driven by the thought of sparing his mother any more pain than one swift flourish of the sharpest steel would cause. His mind had found a way out in putting off, at least temporarily, the most sinful act of killing one's mother. Days rolled by, but the instrument was not yet ready.

In the meantime, while the elder sage was in the forests, he received a providential revelation about the innocence of his wife. Deeply regretting the hasty decision he had made, the sage rushed back to the hermitage.

Cirakārī prostrated before his father, who saw his frail wife in the background and realized that she had not been executed after all. Overcome by joy, he hugged both his wife and son, and thanked Cirakārī for saving him from imminent sin that could have haunted him life after life, all because of a hasty decision. The sage praised his son for deferring the execution, thus preventing an unpardonable error on his own part, and lauded the young ascetic's wisdom in letting serious contemplation take precedence over action.

This story is not just about the necessity of deliberation, it also reveals how providence comes to our help when due sensitivity is exercised in critical issues that haunt the mind for a verdict. I had been sitting on the fence, contemplating the path I should take in life. Luckily for me, the divine hand had appeared in the form of Amma, who is verily Mother Pārvatī, to claim me for Herself. Amma is both the means and the end of spirituality. Even to meet someone of this stature is itself a great blessing.

I was becoming restless, my mind already formulating the most expeditious steps to an early changeover. The sparks of an action plan soon grew into a raging fire of yearning to follow Amma, a blaze consuming my inner core. In my mind of minds, I had resolved to take the plunge; there was no turning back for me. I knew that the path of spiritual inquiry and eventual Self-realization had been ordained for me. "We cannot see things that stare us in the face until the hour comes that the mind is ripened" (Ralph Waldo Emerson).

The *Nārada Bhakti Sūtras* unambiguously declares that the rare occurrence of a realized soul in the form of a great

Master imparts grace and purity to people at large, and bestows bliss on departed souls and the celestials. Such a Master becomes a vehicle for upholding dharma.

> *Mōdantē pitarō nṛtyanti dēvatāḥ sanāthā cēyam bhūrbhavati*
>
> The manes (departed souls) rejoice, the gods dance in joy, and this earth itself gets a spiritual savior. (71)

I was buoyed by the prospect of seeking uncharted spiritual frontiers under this guiding light, Amma.

11

Kaivartakaḥ Kēśavaḥ

There is an old tale about a little girl and her father approaching a narrow bridge over a deep gorge. Trying to protect his daughter from accidentally falling over, he offered his hand to her. Intuitively, the small one said, "No, Dad, you hold my hand."

The puzzled father asked, "What's the difference?"

The girl replied, "If I hold your hand and something

happens to me, chances are that I may let your hand go. But if you hold my hand, I know for sure that no matter what happens, you will never let my hand go."

I was convinced that Amma should grip my hand! That became a priority: meeting Amma again and surrendering myself to Her. At the same time, I was in a quandary over the thought of how to announce my decision at home and to my college-mates. I found myself becoming a loner, not desiring the company of friends, and humming and singing only devotional songs. Seeking contemplative silence more often, increasing the duration of meditation, and spending additional time on prayers at home became routine for me. My appetite to talk about and listen to worldly issues decreased, surprising family members and friends.

As days passed, I felt an inner compulsion to formulate a firm plan for fulfilling my wish to go to Vaḷḷikkāvu and see Amma. I realized that my aunt's support was essential in realizing the desire. While waiting for the right moment to launch my plan, I spent quite a few hours re-reading with renewed interest and insight the biography and teachings of Śrī Rāmakṛṣṇa in the light of my recent experiences with Amma.

The brief opportunity to participate in the activities of that day with Amma had given my life a renewed vigor and a distinctly new perspective from which to observe life. One clear example was the way the portrait of Rāmakṛṣṇa Paramahamsa appeared to me. It used to induce a rare feeling of solemnity that found expression earlier in the form of a few teardrops; now, the sage's gaze seemed to penetrate deep into me, giving me hitherto unseen glimpses of His oceanic compassion and love, the hair and beard adorning His shining countenance adding luster to the view.

Amma has said, "With pure *bhakti* (devotion), there is no difficulty in reaching one's spiritual goal. One should yearningly plead with and cry for the Lord. People remember and worship Śrī Rāmakṛṣṇa even today; such is the greatness of pure and chaste devotion."

The life and outlook of the saint assumed a greater meaning, and the lofty path of bhakti he advocated helped to instill in me a deeper thirst for God. In a similar way, the grandeur of Ādi Śankara's *jñāna* (divine wisdom) inspired in me awe and deference in equal measure. While I had only read the works related to Rāmakṛṣṇa and seen a depiction of the traits and greatness of Jagadguru Śankara in a movie, meeting Amma, the real-life embodiment of both, nourished my faith and bolstered my convictions on the superiority of the spiritual path. When one meets someone he genuinely likes, his face blooms with happiness, and when he thinks about this person, an emotional ardor might even cause his eyes to become moist. If physical objects can yield so much happiness and harmony, how much more felicity can be obtained from awareness of the immutable Self.

As if preordained for me, when I went to my aunt a few days later, I found her preparing to go for Amma's darśan. She asked me if I would like to accompany her. What a God-send! I grabbed the offer right away. We then boarded a bus for Vaḷḷikkāvu. I could not have imagined the enormity of the revelation awaiting me on that maiden visit to the remote coastal village skirting the shore that seemed to stretch to eternity, drowned in the din of the thunderous roars of sea waves.

A native of Māvēlikkara, a scenic region with rolling plains filigreed by streams, canals and other water bodies, I was used to its air and ambience. The area is mainly dependent on its agrarian economy. Thanks to the fertile soil here, coconut, areca nut, cashew and many other cash and plantation crops thrive here, contributing to the general prosperity of the place. The tang from the dancing stalks of paddy and the breathtaking whiffs of the mango, cashew and bullet wood trees enhanced the natural appeal of the lush, green flora. The green carpet of the paddy fields on end, pockets of residential enclaves canopied by coconut trees and other species characteristic of the region, as well as the tiled and thatched houses that peeped through the dense green foliage surrounding them were distinct features of the area. The brisk movements of the local agrarian crowd suggested a purposefulness that animated their lives.

On the few occasions I had to leave this idyll, the passage through coastal stretches would induce a strong urge to hasten back to my native domain, the stench of the sea fauna compounding the lethargy and discomfiture I felt.

The bus ride ended at a nondescript junction at Vaḷḷikkāvu, marked by a few small shelters housing low-key shops providing eats and beverages, and small-time provision stores. That there was a walk of a mile and more towards the seacoast, including the crossing of a river in a small dinghy, made me feel uneasy. The walk to the makeshift jetty took me past small, isolated houses on the side belonging to the fishermen community. Signs of simple living were discernible everywhere. Women folk were working on fibrous coconut pith and drying raw material. The air was dense with the disagreeable smells of dead fish and drying peat.

The short trek was proving to be difficult, and the prospective ride in the small country boat engaged in ferrying people across the water body was causing some anxiety. It was going to be my first time in a boat, and the small vessel in view looked suspect, the water stretch too wide to be ignored, what with likely hidden currents and potential hazards. But the captivating beauty of the banks of the deep blue watercourse—stretching into the distant sea and lined on either side by majestic coconut trees dancing merrily in the sea breeze—and the pale blue evening sky were heartwarming.

When the ride commenced, all my reservations surfaced strongly. As the waves caused the tiny craft to sway in midstream, I panicked despite the cool demeanor of the boatman

skillfully steering his way ahead. In spite of being a lover of natural beauty, I was not too fond of coastal areas then, and this hindered my familiarization with them.

As the boat drifted towards the far bank, a sudden awareness of an invisible power urging me to look ahead in spite of my apprehensive mindset relieved me of all tension. I was reminded of '*Kaivartakaḥ Kēśavaḥ*,' the helmsman Kṛṣṇa, who took the Pāṇḍavas safely across the dangerous river of the Mahābhārata War, and by extension, who maneuvers devotees facing critical situations in life to well-being. In later times, when an incessant flow of devotees would queue up to meet Amma, seeking respite from their innumerable life problems, I beheld Kaivartakaḥ Kēśavaḥ in Her sensitive and spontaneous response, which brought even more of the suffering lot to Her. The lucid mental picture was of Amma taking souls in distress across the threatening straits of '*samsāra*' (cycle of births and deaths) to the shores of eternal safety. The feeling of security I felt in that slender country boat that day made all the more sense when I later came across a photograph of Amma oaring a small craft by Herself.

As if someone had turned on a celestial faucet, a thin radiance, like a spray of gold, appeared from nowhere, illumining my inner senses. Every blade of grass and bead of sand was crystalline as the evening sun flashed on them. The strange and lonesome feeling vanished. I could hardly breathe for awe and joy.

In retrospect, I realize that the wave of sudden joy, which lifted the listlessness that swamped me as I traveled from the plains to the coast, had come from the small hamlet hosting the great Master.

We finally reached Parayakaṭavu, abode of Amma's modest dwelling. The hamlet lies in a linear, tongue-shaped peninsular land formation sandwiched between the scenic Arabian sea and a deep blue river. (With subsequent developments in the region, bridges connecting the area from North and South have made access to the site easy for vehicular traffic. After the devastating tsunami of 2004, Amma's āśram constructed a massive pedestrian bridge that would facilitate a speedy evacuation of the coastal population in the event of another disaster.) We entered the premises of the house where Amma's father, mother and siblings stayed. In its proximity was a small shrine (*'kaḷari'*) in which Amma used to meet Her devotees and give them darśan.

The Malayāḷam word 'kaḷari' originally connoted a place, center or institution that imparted training in martial arts. It also variously denoted a school for education and family shrines instrumental in nourishing a time-honored value system in the young, growing generation. The focus was mainly on cultivating the mind to conform to a behavioral pattern that promoted peace and harmony in society. An immortal verse of Ācārya Śankara in *Śivānanda Laharī* eloquently points out the significance of real learning:

> *vartantē bahuśō mṛgā madajuṣō mātsaryamōhādaya-*
> *stān hatvā mṛgayāvinōda rucitālābham ca samprāpsyasi*
> O Lord, my mind is infested with several untamed, wild animals like desire, anger, envy and delusion. By killing them, you will gain the pleasure of a good hunt. (43)

Here, the Ācārya invokes Lord Śiva in the form of Kirāta, the primeval hunter to cleanse his own mind of the six cardinal enemies[16] masquerading as untamed beasts in the forest of his mind.

---

16 Kāmaḥ—Desire; Krōdhaḥ—Anger; Lōbhaḥ—Greed; Mōhaḥ—Delusion; Madaḥ—Pride; Mātsaryaḥ—Envy.

Just as the martial art form is aimed at spiritual transcendence by disciplining and stretching the disciple's mental and physical resources to ever-new limits, Amma's kaḷari has as its end the Truth, which it helps seekers attain through the means of exercising, honing and burnishing their discriminative intellect in order to overcome the threats posed by inner enemies such as desire, anger and greed.

12

Dwāpara Dusk

It was early in the evening, and Amma was immersed in singing devotional songs in the room where She used to meet devotees. The atmosphere was electric with spiritual fervor, strains of the melodious singing of bhajans wafting from within, captivating my pining mind. As I reached the doorway of the room, I saw Amma sitting with a few devotees, including my brother Bālagōpāl, scoring and rehearsing a devotional song, '*Hṛdayanivāsini Ammē*' ('O Mother, residing in the heart').

The strains of the bhajan captivated my soul, blissfully heralding the Divine Mother's entry into my heart. Its auspicious feel added to the heightened vibrations I felt upon entering the room. My attention was automatically drawn to Amma, who was immersed in a trance, the singing fusing the singer and the song into a single entity. Her rendition of the song, uplifting the moods of those listening, was ambrosia for my soul. I found myself transported to another world, brimming with joy. When the focus shifts from other matters, one naturally becomes merged in oneself.

When that bhajan ended, Amma looked up and saw me. She invited me to come and sit close to Her. After inquiring briefly about my personal welfare, She asked me to join in the singing. Amma also wanted me to lead a bhajan. I sang '*Mangaḷadarśana dāyikē*,' a popular, semi-classical devotional hymn of those times. In Amma's sacred presence, I could feel the subtle impact the song was having on me, a veritable transformation overwhelming me.

A portrait on the wall, depicting the Mother Goddess with a small child seated on Her lap, seemed to reflect splendidly my mental state. The experience of that ecstatic event was just beyond words. By the time I finished singing, I was buoyed by blissful joy. Choking with emotion, I started sobbing like a small child, the emotive strings of my mind unraveling, as it were.

Avidyāhṛdayagranthivimokṣō'pi bhavēdyataḥ
tamēva gururityāhurguruśabdārthvēdinaḥ

> Those who have known the meaning of the word 'Guru' say that He alone who can untie the knot of ignorance in the heart can be called a Guru.
>
> *(Sarvavēdāntasiddhāntasārasangraham, 255)*

Those who were witnessing the scene could intuit my firm resolve to follow the spiritual path, and that there was nothing that would stand in the way of this determination. A trace of worry appeared to crease the face of my brother, probably concerned that another responsible youngster in the family was now planning to sever worldly ties to become a monk, distressing our elders in the bargain.

Amma once said, "A *sādhak* (spiritual seeker) should have the conviction that God will take care of his family. All that is required is unflagging faith in the Lord. Instead of severing attachments, the sādhak should step up efforts to seek the Truth. Cultivate love for God, and all other attachments will automatically fall off."

Amma left the room for the kaḷari, before which She gave darśan to a few devotees standing nearby and waiting for the bhajan session that was to precede the Kṛṣṇa Bhāva[17] later in the evening.

17 While narrating this part, recourse has been taken to address the Kṛṣṇa Bhāva by a number of endearing names, viz., Amṛta Kṛṣṇa, Kṛṣṇa Form, Kṛṣṇa Manifestation and Bhagavān.

She sat in front of the kaḷari along with the bhajan group, surrounded by the devotees gathered there. The program lasted a little more than an hour, concluding at around 6:30 p.m. Of the bhajans sung that evening, the one that swept me away on the waves of devotion was, '*Ammē bhagavatī nityakanyē*,' Amma's soulful rendition of the lyrics saturating the environment altogether. Amma then got up and went inside the kaḷari (also called the '*Kṛṣṇan Naṭa*,' meaning 'Kṛṣṇa Temple'), accompanied by a few female devotees, after which the doors of the shrine closed behind them.

About 15 minutes later, the doors reopened, and I saw Amma singing a devotional song to Kṛṣṇa. A serene ambience set in, and the doors to the kaḷari closed a little later.

Becoming a little curious about what was going to happen next, I asked a devotee standing nearby, "Now what?"

In a voice touched by piety, he replied, "When the door opens, you can see Bhagavān[18] Kṛṣṇa."

My thoughts found their way to Vṛndāvan, Mathura and Dwāraka, places hallowed by the Lord's association, recalling the thematic highs of Kṛṣṇa's life and the events that glorified this great incarnation.

---

18 "Bhagam yasyāsti saḥ Bhagavān," i.e. Bhagavān (the Lord) is one who is endowed with the six attributes called 'bhagam.' According to Viṣṇu Purāṇam, "Aiśvaryasya samagrasya vīryasya yaśasaḥ śriyaḥ jñānavairāgyayōścaiva ṣaṇṇām bhaga itīritāḥ" (6.5.74)—Bhagam comprises supremacy, valor, fame, prosperity, knowledge and dispassion.

Amma and Kṛṣṇa are two sides of the same coin. Kṛṣṇa personifies the chastest form of the human mind, and the subtlest essence of dharma. He distinguishes Himself as an unsurpassed celebrity of the *Mahābhārata* and the *Bhāgavatam* who accepted life as a whole, despite its endless vagaries and distractions. He showed that life was meant for liberation from its illusory designs. In whatever role He chose to play, Kṛṣṇa smiled, laughed and danced through life, demonstrating the ease and equilibrium that can be sustained in the world of dualities—the opposites, and the dark and lighter shades of life. Kṛṣṇa is a phenomenon, a perfect model of integrated completeness.

The melodious flute symbolizes the joy and happiness that Kṛṣṇa bestowed on all those who craved to listen to Him playing the instrument. The Lord played the flute for the sheer love that gladdened the hearts of those who bee-lined to hear the divine music. Goodness spreads like wild fire. Playing a flute entails pursed lips, supple fingers, a singing and dancing heart, and a soul brimming with joy and happiness.

Amma once said, "An ordinary actor confines himself to a small stage, but for Kṛṣṇa, the entire world was His playhouse. He played various characters, the costumes kept changing, and yet the Lord excelled, abiding firmly in the awareness that He was none of these characters but the Supreme Consciousness. In this way, Kṛṣṇa made His own life as well as the lives of those around Him joyous."

Kṛṣṇa was impeccable in His character, conduct and attitude. His life stands as an eternal message to anyone and everyone born and to be born in the future. Although He played His roles in the concluding phase of the *Dwāpara Yuga*,[19] His life was so lustrous as to shed light on the more complex age to come, the *Kali Yuga*, with all its characteristic vicissitudes, so that we may learn from the innumerable examples He set.

Kṛṣṇa demonstrated a sustained equipoise through numerous life situations, whether joyful or sorrowful. He became the worthiest role model for all times to come. Only someone of His exalted caliber could transform the battlefield of Kurukṣētra into an arena for dispensing *Brahmavidyā*, knowledge of the Absolute, to His chosen disciple Arjuna.

In the light of contemporary morality, Kṛṣṇa, with His many wives, children and grandchildren, might seem to be anything but righteous despite His constant and continued

19 According to Hindu cosmogony, the universe passes through four yugas (epochs), namely Kṛta, Trētā, Dwāpara and Kali. Lord Kṛṣṇa incarnated during the Dwāpara Yuga.

endeavors to uphold dharma. He may be seen as husband and lover to a number of women, as having indulged in deceptive strategies to defeat his antagonists, and as one who instilled fear in the minds of His enemies. Yet He was acknowledged and acclaimed throughout Bhāratam as *Śrī Kṛṣṇa Paramātma*—Śrī Kṛṣṇa, the Supreme Being. Each of His actions bore definite objectives, reflected clarity of thought, and revealed purity of execution, all of which stemmed from profound awareness. Devotees intuit this, thus valorizing jñāna over karma. People then were generally aware that spiritual Masters were unaffected by karma and detached from it. In Kṛṣṇa's words, "*Sarvabhūtātmabhutatma kurvannapi na lipyate*" (*Bhagavad Gītā*, 5.7) ("He who has identified himself with the Self of all beings remains unattached even when he performs actions"). The esteem in which Lord Kṛṣṇa is held speaks highly of the extent to which scriptural insight has percolated into the lives of traditional Indians.

Peace encompasses the elements of harmony, freedom and justice. It cannot be wished for or imposed on anyone. Peace has to arise naturally from adherence to spiritual principles. When Kṛṣṇa, the charming and multi-faceted personality, administered justice, it resonated at the individual, social and universal realms. Never negating any natural progression, He clearly showed the middle path, discouraging indulgence in extremes. This was the dominant feature of the time-honored outlook on living, which was another reason that compelled the saints and sages of the past to acknowledge Kṛṣṇa's wisdom.

Once, one of Amma's devotees asked me, "Swāmiji, aren't there people who criticize Kṛṣṇa for having many wives?"

I humorously replied, "Those who rue the want of many wives and are at the same time envious of Kṛṣṇa for having them are the ones who complain thus!"

The desire to win can take one into the battleground of victory or defeat. Seen from a dispassionate point of view, Kṛṣṇa was never bent on any conquest; He symbolized utter desirelessness. Lao Tzu, father of Taoism, once told his friends, "No one could defeat me all my life."

Before he could continue, one of his friends interrupted him, "Please tell us how you managed to become invincible?"

On hearing this, Lao Tzu laughed and said, "You will not understand it as you lack patience, since I was about to explain why. I was going to say that no one could defeat me because I am already defeated; no one could defeat me since I never wanted to win."

Humility is vital. To admit defeat in spirituality is to succeed eventually. This does not mean that we give up our efforts to attain Liberation, but that we surrender our ambition. One who has no ambition can never fail; one who never fails always succeeds; and one who always succeeds is all-powerful.

13

Divine Darśan

In the meantime, I gathered that Amma was donning the attire of Kṛṣṇa. The atmosphere was comparable to the ambience that prevails in any important temple shrine. The devotee crowd, charged with piety, thronged either side of the narrow aisle leading to the main entrance of the temple, and an air of expectancy hung over them as they waited for their deity to make His divine appearance.

The shrine doors opened to reveal *ārati*[20] being performed to Amma in Kṛṣṇa garb. The punctuated ringing of the bronze bells and the clarion call of the conch intermingled to create a mystical aura. The glow of the traditional brass lamps enhanced the sense of sanctity. The incense sticks wafted their sweet, captivating scent, enriching the super-charged ambience with their redolence.

20 Clockwise movement of a lamp to propitiate a deity.

Amma emerged, dressed in a yellow robe, brilliantly bejeweled in bangles, anklets and rings, and wearing a peacock-feather-plumed golden-colored crown. Her benign smiling countenance and the majestic stance—left foot gracefully lifted and placed on a low pedestal, the right palm exhibiting the '*jñānamudrā*'[21] and the left palm artfully bent, denoting refuge—personified Lord Kṛṣṇa profoundly, an identity conforming to the persona conceived of in the minds of devotees. Amma's body was continuously throbbing, and Her left leg, resting on the pedestal, vibrated synchronically with the gentle shaking of the body. The sight was so overwhelming and awe-inspiring that onlookers were relieved of body consciousness, at least temporarily.

The devout, charged with spiritual fervor, began soulfully chanting "*Kṛṣṇa!*" "*Kṛṣṇa!*" "*Bhagavānē!*" and a few of them threw themselves headlong in prostration on the ground. Soon, the crowd began forming a queue for Amma's darśan. I could gauge the mood of the devotees by now; to them, this was Kṛṣṇa Himself waiting to meet them individually.

To me, this experience was new. It brought my analytical mind to the fore. Being an over-zealous, single-minded Kṛṣṇa devotee from my earliest childhood, I regarded Him as the Supreme Lord of the Universe. My mind had been

21 *The mystic gesture of knowledge: the index finger is bent so that its tip is joined with the tip of the thumb, with the other three fingers spread out.*

led to believe that His form was ever unique and could not have a second to replace or replicate it. It was difficult to reconcile myself to this scenario where a young woman had transformed herself to soulfully portray Kṛṣṇa, the Lord of lords.

My confused mind, perturbed by preconceived notions, was unable to come to terms with the reality in front of me. The mind caught in the web of inertia refuses to acknowledge plain facts. This flaw of the mind, the veil of ignorance, is "a kind of optical delusion of consciousness," in Einstein's words.

I was in a dilemma, wondering how all the energy had materialized in this young lady, transforming Her into a model of the great Lord. "How is it possible?" was the question turning over in my mind, which was struggling to come to terms with the manifestation I was witnessing now, a version so much endorsed by the huge devotee crowd!

Once, a devotee asked Amma a question: "Isn't Amma a divine incarnation? If this were true, what is the relevance of the Kṛṣṇa and Dēvī Manifestations?"

Amma replied, "The devotees have their own perspective of the name and form of their personal deities like Rāma, Kṛṣṇa and Dēvī, although they are all manifestations of the same unifying consciousness. Amma wanted to reach Her devotees in the forms dear to them."

For an all-knowing, all-pervading Master like Amma, it is easy to assume the form dearest to the devotee, an indication also of the overwhelming love and compassion that is so natural and integral to Her divine nature!

In my unsolicited haste to plunge into a comparison of these two great souls of two different time periods and life settings, I had overlooked the fact that Kṛṣṇa lived more than 5,000 years ago, the recalling of His hallowed life immeasurably enriched by historical perspective, millennia of adoration, and the collective force of legend and myth, whereas Amma was a newly arisen sun in the spiritual firmament, a contemporary in Her mid-20s. It was sheer foolishness to compare the two. I looked forward to the next phase of the Kṛṣṇa Darśan.

The devotees formed two separate queues, one for males and the other for females, to move into Amma's arms to get Her darśan. Amma's darśan is unique in many ways. 'Darśan' literally means 'to see.' Traditionally, a Master is only seen but not touched, and least of all hugged. The darśan of Amma is Her concept—the awareness that all are one—uniquely adapted to reality, Her mission informed by Her vision.

I also followed suit and joined the queue. As I was about to step over the threshold of the Kṛṣṇan Naṭa, I heard my aunt who had accompanied me whispering into my ears,

"Remember to prostrate at Bhagavān's feet." I could see that devotees were paying obeisance in diverse ways: some were prostrating fully with arms stretched out to touch Amma's feet; and some were going down on their knees and bowing their heads down at Her feet in total surrender.

As I closed in on Amma, I felt that I was being suffused by the divine aura of Her Kṛṣṇa Form. With the devotee in my front finishing his darśan and breaking away from the queue, I found myself face to face with Amma. Despite the recent encounter with divinity, I was still caught in the web of my internal thought processes about the fullness of the Kṛṣṇa Manifestation, and all I could manage was to bend over slightly and touch Amma's knees with my hands and bring them to my forehead.

14

Spiritual Sunrise

I was looking at Amma as She looked directly into my eyes. I don't know how long I was caught in Her mesmerizing gaze. The color of Amma's eyes resembled the deep blue hue of the unending sky. Those orbs cast a magic spell and transported me to Vṛndāvan, abode of the wondrous tales of Kṛṣṇa. There was in Her enchanting beam a striking similarity to the captivating, all-knowing smile of my Kṛṣṇa.

Amma then took me into Her arms and laid my head on Her shoulder, clasping me in one hand while gently caressing my back with the other, motherly affection and nectarous love bathing me in divine bliss! With my head resting on Amma's incredibly comforting shoulder, I could feel a delicate, beguiling fragrance slowly overpowering me, a scent that could not be attributed to any earthly flower or perfume. The mind appeared weightless, floating like a free cloud, unburdened. My eyes suddenly became moist; I don't know why. In those sublime moments, all I could remember was my heart thirsting for the waters of pure love, devotion and knowledge.

Once, later in my life, a reporter asked me, "How did you feel when you met Amma?"

My answer spontaneously took the form of another question. "What do you feel when you see the morning sun at dawn? Can you really describe the experience?"

I was hardly aware of the passage of time as I lay my head on Amma's shoulder until She lifted my head gently with Her right palm, and moved my head to face Her. I found myself unable to speak, the mind ensconced in a blissful warmth that permeated my inner core, leaving me entranced. The silence was eventually broken by Amma as She spoke: *"Kombā nī entu tēṭi alayunnuvō, Amma atu mōnu kāṇiccutarām"*—"Son, whatever you have been seeking in your wanderings, Amma will show it to you!" The Guru is one who has climbed and reached the highest stage, from where He can distinctly see the rungs.

Saying so, Amma took me once more into Her arms, and as She hugged me with Her characteristic love and affection, She whispered a mantra into my ear.

When She released me from Her divine hug, I found the solace that had been eluding me, a state of undefined happiness taking over and erasing all hidden anxieties, bracing me for my quest in life.

15

Testing Time

I found myself reflecting on the experience. Strangely, the sequence of events in my life had culminated in meeting Amma, whose promise to take me to the goal assured me that I would realize a childhood dream rooted in my intense devotion to Kṛṣṇa. This current of devotion had gained momentum from the movie on Ācārya Śankara, and reached sublime heights after meeting Amma.

Through this guarantee, Amma, personifying the Guru principle in the garb of Kṛṣṇa, was showing Her oneness with all of creation, thus underscoring its underlying unity. All the forms, figures and names in my mind merged into one, which I perceived and addressed as Amma, the Guru, who is the one who reveals the nature of the 'I' in me. Under Her guidance, my pilgrimage to the Truth was going to be eventful.

Amma placed Her forefinger, which was dipped in sandal paste, on the center of my forehead for a while, anointing and energizing me simultaneously. She then gave me a garland of fresh basil leaves and an incense stick, and indicating a place in Her proximity, directed me to sit there and meditate until the incense stick was burned out.

I sat down on the floor and, with eyes closed, tried to meditate as directed by Amma. However much I tried to concentrate, the thought of comparing the Kṛṣṇa Form with the model of the Lord in my mind began to torment me. In spite of the conviction I had gained from experience, the doubt about whether Amma could be as great as Kṛṣṇa continued to nag me. As soon as the thought reared its head the first time, I experienced a gentle touch on my chin; it was Amma rousing me from my assessing with the words, "*Enna ḍā?*" ("What son?").

I continued meditating, making a conscious effort to resist the doubts, but they crept in again sooner than later. The moment the thought reappeared, I felt a nudge on my chin. It was Amma again repeating, "*Enna ḍā?*"

This happened a couple of times more, to my great surprise each time! However, my mind, slowly coming to grips with the reality, was in a mood to test the Master's omniscience. I thought, "If only Amma would feed me the holy milk kept in the bronze *kiṇṭi* (metal water pot with a snout) by Her side." Lo! I felt something touching my lips, and on opening my eyes, found the snout of the kiṇṭi touching my lips, Amma Herself feeding me the milk! Unbelievable though it was, my mind still tried to count this as a remarkable coincidence, and wagered if this would repeat again upon my wish. Amma yet again decanted drops of milk through the vessel's snout directly into my mouth immediately on the occurrence of the thought.

I went back to meditating. Before long, my analytical mind was once again hot on the trail to find one last proof of the greatness of this Master. The glory of my personal deity, Lord Kṛṣṇa, was continuing to dominate my thoughts, inwardly compelling me to seek confirmation of the equivalence between Kṛṣṇa and Amma. In a flash, I thought to myself, "If this form is really Kṛṣṇa in substance, the personal deity that I have been worshipping with all faith and devotion until this day, let these hands give me a part of the offering used in the worship that day." Barely had the thought entered my mind that I felt something pressing against my lips. Opening my eyes one more time, I found Amma trying to gently push a piece of plantain into my mouth! The cut pieces of plantain, being the offering to the deity, had already been kept by Amma's side. This amazed me to no end but my mind still compelled me to accept it only as mere happenstance.

My mind continued to demand proof yet again as I closed my eyes and attempted to meditate. I did not have to wait longer than a few moments after the thought marched past, before I opened my eyes to the touch of a fresh plantain piece on my lips! Despite the proof I got this time to negate my nagging doubt, I found my mind coaxing me to consider this, too, as another instance of sheer coincidence.

My unbelieving mind craved for proof one more time. The intensity of devotion with which I had been worshipping Kṛṣṇa from my early childhood was obviously affecting my judgment and consequently preventing my acceptance of this repeated proof. No sooner had I wished for fresh proof a third time than Amma, Amṛta Kṛṣṇa, touched my lips with a piece of plantain, rousing me from meditation.

Awestruck, I ate the plantain. The curtains had finally fallen on my doubts. Amṛta Kṛṣṇa, the cosmic phenomenon, needed no further testing by a mere earthling! It is a great folly to think that what we do not perceive is non-existent.

Saccidānandarūpaya viswotpatyādihētavē
Tāpatrayavināśāya Śrīkṛṣṇāya vayam numaḥ

We bow down to Lord Kṛṣṇa who is of the nature of Existence-Knowledge-Bliss absolute, the cause of the universe, its preservation and dissolution and who ends the three-fold sorrow (of beings).

(Bhāgavata Māhātmyam, 1.1)

Viśvangaḷellāmuḷavākki munnam
Viśvāsapūrvam parirakṣaceytum
Niśśēṣamanpōṭatha samhariccum

Niśśokamōdam viḷayaṭuvon nī

O Lord, You playfully create the universe at the beginning, then safely sustain it, and finally destroy it in toto, without grief or joy.

(Śrīkṛṣṇacaritam Maṇipravāḷam, 2.8)

The human mind, benighted by ignorance, often blindly probes the greatness of elevated souls established in the Supreme Truth. I was guilty of this misdemeanor. But one thing is obvious: ignorance cannot prevail; only true knowledge triumphs in the final analysis.

The *Muṇḍakōpaniṣad* extols: "*Satyamēva jayatē nānṛtam*" (3.1.6), meaning "Truth alone triumphs, not untruth." Although the Guru is a sure winner, the disciple's victory lies in his own defeat, i.e. in the vanquishing of his ego.

A devotee once asked me, "Swāmiji, why do some people leave the āśram after staying there for so many years?"

I replied, "It is because they have no desire for *mōkṣa* (spiritual liberation), and instead harbor desires for worldly objects. In order to fulfill them, they leave the āśram. None of them do so to dedicate their lives to spirituality. Instead, they immerse themselves in materialism."

Those who left had sung paeans to Amma's love and compassion while they were in the āśram; these very people then criticize Her when they are unable to fulfill their personal

desires. In spite of these fluctuations in their attitude, Amma has remained ever the same, Her love continuing to flow to all, sans discrimination.

In truth, Amma is not affected by people's arrival to or departure from the āśram. There is an interesting anecdote concerning Albert Einstein during his early school days.

Once, when he made a mistake in solving a math problem, the teacher asked him, "Don't you know that in subtraction, the result is always something less?"

Einstein replied, "Not always, madam. How about the two ends of a stick? Cut them both off and still we will have two ends left!"

In the same way, the āśram's stature is not diminished in any way when residents, even long-time ones, leave. By the same logic, Amma's glory is not enhanced in any way by the advent of new people into the āśram. The following verse from the *Gītā* describes the serene state of a mahātma like Amma:

> *apūryamāṇamacalaḥ pratiṣṭham*
> *samudramāpaḥ praviśanti yadvat*
> *tadvat kāmā yam praviśanti sarvē*
> *sa śāntimāpnōti na kāmakāmī*
>
> A person who is not disturbed by the incessant flow of desires—that enter like rivers into the ocean, which is ever being filled but is always still—alone can achieve peace, and not the man who strives to satisfy such desires. (2.70)

Many years ago, Amma had told me, "Thousands may come and thousands may leave. However, I've depended always only on one thing: the Unchanging Reality."

16

Selfsame Soul

I was reflecting on the general picture I had in my mind before coming here: that this young woman had some supernatural powers when She transformed Herself into Kṛṣṇa and Dēvī by which She was able to heal the afflicted, read the future, and bestow boons on devotees. My testing of Amma had silenced my cynical mind, removing all traces of doubt about Her omniscience.

All claims to disbelief are hollow. When one says that he does not believe someone or something, he believes that 'disbelief.' Therefore, one way or the other, faith is the basis of belief or disbelief.

In the *Viṣṇu Sahasranāmastōtram* (1,000 names of Lord Viṣṇu), the Lord is extolled as "*Ātmayōniḥ svayamjātō...*" ("The uncaused Cause, the Self-born") (119), i.e., the all-inclusive. How strange it was that this young woman revealing the Kṛṣṇa Manifestation had kindled in me the conviction that She was the sum and substance of that male incarnation of the Dwāpara Yuga. I did not have even a shadow of doubt that the two were different manifestations of the same cosmic entity.

Amma's reassurance in guiding me to the goal ("*Amma atu mōnu kāṇiccutarām*") was astounding, suggesting that She was an authentic incarnation. This conviction emerged when I was trying to piece together the gross aspect of what I saw in Amṛta Kṛṣṇa and the subtle import of what I heard from Her. Another piece of the mosaic was laid by Amma's responses to my earlier doubts on meditation, which revealed Her omniscience. A clear picture was beginning to emerge.

Here was Amma, responding in the inimitable manner of Bhagavān: "Amma will take care" of my quest of the spiritual goal. The significant point is the reference to Amma while in the garb of Bhagavān Kṛṣṇa. In this, we see the boundaries between the two divine forms evaporating into thin air.

I soon realized the import of Amma's mystic utterance: that the Amma of the Kṛṣṇa Manifestation and the Amma of the Dēvī Manifestation were facets of the same unifying consciousness, the Universal Mother. In a flash, the significance of the word 'Kṛṣṇa' struck me: it was the name of the male Lord Kṛṣṇa *and* the female Goddess Kāḷī ('Kṛṣṇā').

On reflection, I marveled at how fortunate I was to have opted to pursue my college studies at Māvēlikkara when there were other alternatives open in nearby towns. It gave me an opportunity to visit occasionally my aunt (an ardent devotee of Amma), who was residing close by.

My grandmother, who had a major influence on my upbringing during my childhood days, was an ardent Kṛṣṇa devotee. Her prayer room had only one portrait: that of Lord Kṛṣṇa. However, the family's long-standing association with the famous Cheṭṭikuḷangara Bhagavatī Temple[22] kept her involved with matters and activities of this great shrine to Dēvī. Although I inherited the single-deity (Lord Kṛṣṇa) culture from my grandmother, the familial association with the Bhagavatī temple was instrumental in propelling me eventually into Amma's fold.

22 This temple shrine has been mentioned in different contexts in the course of the narration; it has been referred to variously as Local Dēvī Shrine, Bhagavatī Temple, Family Deity and Bhadrakāḷī Temple.

"*Yathā karma yathā śrutam*" (*Kaṭhōpaniṣad*, 2.2.7)—one's actions and knowledge determine one's destiny, i.e. one's future births. My single-minded devotion to Lord Kṛṣṇa notwithstanding, some of the features of Dēvī worship made a deep impression on my young mind, such as the thrill I felt on hearing the popular invocation to the Divine Mother in Her dynamic, ferocious form, which we used to sing: "*Dēvi dēvi dayānidhē! Pāhi pāhi bhadrakāḷi!*"

Devotees used to address Amma as "*Bhagavānē*" in Kṛṣṇa Form; as "*Ammachi*" or "*Dēvi Amma*" in Dēvī Bhāva; and as "*Kuññē*" or "*Ammachi-kuññē*" (a term of endearment meaning 'child') at other times. The realization—dawning on me in the very first meeting with Amma in Vaḷḷikkāvu—that these are different facets of the same entity, the Universal Mother, is attributable to the immense grace of the Guru.

The Guru is the 'inner eye' with which one can behold the Absolute principle. Our outer organs of vision are not ideal for looking within; what is needed is insight based on conviction and single-minded focus. "*Antarādantarōsmyaham*" (2.18) of *Maitrēyōpaniṣad* eloquently states that the '*Ātma*' (soul) is in the innermost recesses of the heart. Earnestness in spirituality is nothing but the yearning for the Ātma. One who has no self-confidence will find it difficult to have faith in Amma.

The seeker on the trail of Truth must become familiar with the path. If we are not familiar with it, we need the help of a guide. A Guru is one who knows the ins and outs of the mind in all its subtlety. Just as we seek the help of an intermediary to introduce us to a stranger we wish to meet, we need the help of a Guru to familiarize ourselves with our own minds. Only then can we begin learning how to control the mind. This is the relevance of the Master or Guru.

The normal practice is for Amma to intone the mantra in the ear only during the Dēvī Manifestation. However, on a couple of occasions, on my insistence or rather obstinacy stemming from a lack of insight, Amma had graciously intoned Kṛṣṇa mantras into my ear during the Kṛṣṇa Bhāva darśan. Obsessed with my iṣṭa dēvata, I had even ignored the Master's right to decide on the mantra.

Later, after a year, a deep desire led me to seek from Amma a Kṛṣṇa mantra during a Dēvī Bhāva darśan, conforming to the conventional practice of Amma giving mantra-*dīkṣa* (holy initiation, sometimes involving rituals) only during such occasions. Granting my wish, Amma initiated me formally into a Kṛṣṇa mantra, but told me, "Son, you will ultimately seek Dēvī Herself." Amma had given in to my whim out of maternal affection. However, realized Masters know what is good for us, and so will ultimately act according to what we need, not what we like.

Amma's prophetic words baffled me then, but in the course of time, the relevance of the Dēvī principle started dawning on me, opening new vistas in my spiritual contemplation, and culminating in the gradual realization of the ultimate unity of the Kṛṣṇa and Dēvī forms in this cosmic phenomenon, Amma.

The mind, in its euphoria, was trying to comprehend the sanctity of this great moment of revelation, against the backdrop of my intense devotion for Lord Kṛṣṇa, which I had cultivated over the early years at home, thanks to the profound spiritual ambience created by my grandmother and the elders in the family.

While a few occasions in my life had indirectly given me the feel of the Lord's divine presence, I had not expected to experience His overwhelming physical presence in Amṛta Kṛṣṇa, who set me on the path to realization. If not for the deep, prayerful yearning for His physical presence, I wondered if this could have been possible.

Among the personal experiences of my early life, one of the most memorable was a dream that featured a mysterious incident. It had all the flourishes of a phantasmagoric setting and could have been dismissed as hallucinatory, yet was as clear as daylight. This dream incident, which took place when I was about 12, unfolded in the cropped paddy fields adjacent to my house. Each year, following the harvest cutting, these fields became an ideal playground for children of all ages.

In this lucid dream, my friends and I were immersed in a game one late afternoon, when our attention was suddenly flagged by the rousing hoof-beats of an approaching stallion mounted by a youthful rider. I soon made out that the yellow-robed equestrian, a resplendent warrior with a benign expression and holding aloft an unsheathed sword in his right hand, was expertly guiding the galloping horse towards us.

On the spur of the moment, my playmates ran away while I remained, drawn by the grandeur of the vision. As the steed halted near me, the shining youth dismounted. He bent low, clasped me in a pleasant hug with his left hand, and intoned a message, as if a counsel, into my ear before remounting the horse and riding away!

Reflecting on the incident several times later, I discerned a striking similarity in the outline and gait of this angelic combatant horseman with the form of my iṣṭa-dēvata Kṛṣṇa, who used to appear in my dreams.

Spiritual aspirants naturally come by many experiences, which might give them much bliss. They may even take pride in these experiences, imagining them to be the sole measure of spiritual progress. However, the real Experience—the state of desirelessness—is beyond all phenomenal experience, however blissful; it is union with the Ātma. Whereas most people *assess* life in the light of past experiences, the Illumined *behold* life in the light of the *Experience*. There are not many who seek the Ātma. People can often be heard saying that they have no time for spiritual pursuits. This showy claim to busyness has become their business, its sole profit being creating the impression of being busy. Sadly, the busyness is never with oneself; it is always with belongings and not with what truly belongs to them—the Self.

According to the scriptures, great Masters are personifications of supreme knowledge; scriptural texts merely act as guides to the goal of realization. The *Śvētāśvatarōpaniṣad* is explicit when it says, "*Yastanna vēda kimṛcā kariṣyati*" (4.8)—"Of what use is the Vēda to him who does not know the Indestructible Being (*Akṣara*)?" "Scriptural texts are merely *granthis* (knots of ignorance)," commented Śrī Rāmakṛṣṇa Paramahamsa on the dry, scholastic approach, bereft of sensitivity and devotion, to accepting these texts as authority.

Readers may be familiar with Kabīr, a great mystic, thinker, philosopher and poet. He was known far and wide for his spiritual insight and his extraordinary personality.

Stories abound of his honesty, forthrightness, humility, single-minded devotion to God, and compassion to fellow beings. An anecdote from Kabīr's life features a pundit who had studied deeply the scriptural texts, and was well-known for his erudition. The pundit prided himself on this fact, and chose for himself the title '*Sarbajīt*,' meaning 'one who has won over all others.'

On completion of his formal studies, Sarbajīt returned home and boasted about his learning to his mother, and insisted that she call him by the name he had assumed. The mother said that she would do so if he could demonstrate that his knowledge surpassed that of Kabīr. "Oh, that is nothing, I will go through that formality in no time," said the son, and hurried off to the poet-saint's humble dwelling.

The saint welcomed the scholar and asked, "Well, Punditji,[23] what brings you here?" The latter introduced himself by the honorary name he had chosen, and informed Kabīr that he had come to establish his superiority to Kabīr in knowledge. The sage smiled and told him that there was no need for any argument, and agreed to sign any certification the young scholar wanted. Pleased with this turn of events, the pundit wrote down what he wanted on a paper and asked the celebrated poet to sign it.

23 'Ji' is an honorific denoting respect.

Reaching home, he showed the paper to his mother, who took it and read aloud, "Sarbajīt has lost and Kabīr has won!"

Disbelieving, he read it for himself and said, "How is this possible? There must be some mistake. I will go back and get it corrected."

On arriving at the saint's house, he blurted out, "Mahārāj,[24] I made a slight mistake. I want to rewrite the paper." The latter amiably agreed, and signed the new declaration.

When the pundit reached home, his mother read the paper and exclaimed, "But there is no change! It is the same as it was earlier!"

In frustration, the scholar shouted, "I will go back once again," and hurried off.

Great Masters never belittle a person. Instead, they make them understand with love. In all earnestness, Kabīr pointed out to the pundit, "How can you think only of winning, without wanting to realize the truth involved? I speak what I have seen and experienced, whereas your viewpoint is exclusively based on what you have read." God is a mere concept for the ignorant; He is an experience for the wise. Most ignoramuses are endowed with two 'assets:' an utter lack of awareness and ignorance about it. In the absence of

24 Literally, 'great king;' a term used for addressing a saintly person.

real wisdom, the least that is required of us is to be aware of our ignorance. Whereas the accomplished reveal their strength by refraining from demonstrating their prowess, the imperfect betray their incompetence by trying to show off their hollow ability.

When the greatness of Masters is doubted or when their superiority is challenged by bloated egos deluded by narrow worldly knowledge, these spiritual giants, displaying their characteristic humility, make us realize the truth through acts that become our own life experiences.

17

Lordly Līlās

Continuing to sit by Amma's side, I was able to get a ringside view of darśan, the teeming devotees lining up one by one. Among this variegated crowd, many were concerned about the health and well-being of their near and dear ones; some were seeking blessings for the realization of material prosperity and affluence; and a few were driven purely by their unflinching admiration for and devotion to Amṛta Kṛṣṇa.

Among the pullulating mass of devotees, the constant was the heart-warming sight of Amṛta Kṛṣṇa. To each one who came to Her, She responded with sustained love and care, and an all-knowing, compassionate gaze that had the power to heal the mental wounds of the afflicted, providing unconditional hope to the seeker and enthusing the devout. Those craving special boons received a stock answer: "You request Śakti," directing them to seek it from Dēvī during Dēvī Bhāva, which was soon to follow.

Amṛta Kṛṣṇa's childlike pranks reminded one of Kṛṣṇa's playful acts, like the time a devotee, who was offered a piece of plantain, opened his mouth expecting the prasādam but did not find it forthcoming; Amma had put it into Her own mouth! Another time, when a devotee opened his mouth to receive milk from the kiṇṭi, the flow from the snout of the vessel did not stop, thus spilling out from his mouth, much to the amusement of others.

The most outstanding feature of Kṛṣṇa Bhāva was its mirthful ambience, suggesting the subtle presence of Kṛṣṇa. Memories of His life and līlās, chronicled in Purāṇic tales, seized my mind. Accentuating the Kṛṣṇa līlā was Amma's playful scooping of butter from pots offered by devotees, and good-natured smearing of butter, some of which adorned Her lips and cheeks, on the faces of devotees, all the while wearing a winsome smile so characteristic of the Lord.

On reflection, it was clear that Amṛta Kṛṣṇa was Lord Kṛṣṇa, who always maintained His equipoise. His peerless smile was the constant in the vicissitudes of life. The Lord was free of all attachment, His dispassion a vantage point from which He looked on life.

The Lord's glory is extolled thus in the *Puruṣasūktam*: "*Ētāvānasya mahimā atō jyāyāmśca pūruṣaḥ*" ("All this (the entire universe) is His glory; but He is also above all this").

Soon after the extraordinary incident involving Amma feeding me plantain pieces every time I thought of gauging Her power of omniscience, and the alluring display of Her Kṛṣṇa līlā, all the devotees were geared to watch Amma dance in Kṛṣṇa Form, a dance preceding Her Dēvī Manifestation. Later, in Her Dēvī garb, Amma would dance for a considerable period of time in the immediate vicinity of the kaḷari, and away into the enveloping darkness in and around the outskirts of the kaḷari. The *nṛtta līlā* (divine dance form) of Amṛta Kṛṣṇa was relatively briefer and performed only in the immediate front of the kaḷari.

Many enigmatic occurrences unfolded during Kṛṣṇa darśan. The following incident, which is still talked about by those who had the good fortune to witness it, emphasizes the profundity of Amma's love and concern for Her devotees. It also reveals Her omniscience. The mystical acts of great Masters should not be seen as instances of self-glorification; they are intended to strengthen the faith of devotees.

On that day, the *nṛtta* (dance) exceeded the usual period of time and, at one point, looked as if it would continue unceasingly, much to the amazement of the devotees. However, it stopped abruptly at the arrival of a regular devotee. This person, who had set out early from his home for the Amṛta Kṛṣṇa darśan, was delayed on the way and could reach the kaḷari only then. Amma had clearly been waiting for him.

However, the significant part of this incident was the fact that he had been carrying a small parcel of home-made flaked rice intended as a special offering to Amma. This humble offering rekindles the memory of Sudāma, Kṛṣṇa's childhood chum and fellow student at Sage Sāndīpani's *gurukula.*[25] The story has it that they parted company at the end of their schooling and did not meet again until Sudāma called on Kṛṣṇa at Dwāraka, His abode, decades later with a small offering of flattened rice.

The Lord, thrilled by the prospect of seeing His childhood pal after a long time, hurried out of his royal chambers, even forgetting to put on His footwear, much to the astonishment of His consort Rukmiṇī Dēvī.

> *Mudā gamiccāśu kucēlavipran*
> *Mukundagēhattinakattupukkān*
> *Varunnakaṇṭambujanētranappōḷ*
> *Karampiṭiccangarikattirutti*
>
> Kucēla (Sudāma), the Brahmin, soon entered Śrī Kṛṣṇa's palace with a happy heart. The lotus-eyed Lord, seeing Kucēla advancing towards Him, took His friend's hand in His own and made him sit next to Him.
>
> *(Śrīkṛṣṇacaritam Maṇipravāḷam, 12.15)*

The story symbolizes the reunion of the *Jīvātma* (individual soul) and *Paramātma* (Supreme Being), the overwhelming

25 Literally, the clan (kula) of the preceptor (Guru); traditional school where students would stay with the Guru for the entire duration of their scriptural studies.

devotion of Kucēla (the Jīvātma) uniting him with Lord Kṛṣṇa (the Paramātma). *Bhaja-gōvindam* is explicit: "*Tvayi mayi cānyatraikō Viṣṇuḥ*" ("The selfsame (all-pervasive) Viṣṇu dwells in you, in me and in all others and in everything else"). A similarly unambiguous thought from the *Kaṭhōpaniṣad* is noteworthy: "*Nēha nānāsti kiñcana*" (2.1.11) ("Here, there is no diversity at all").

18

Numinous Nṛtta

The narration of events relating to Amṛta Kṛṣṇa will not be complete unless I include this interesting episode, which happened in the āśram one day during the early years. Amma was in a mood for debate, unusual for Her, and at one point, started playing the devil's advocate. She picked on my Kṛṣṇa fixation to drive home a few philosophical truths. The traits of Kṛṣṇa, regarded as sacrosanct by the devout, were the butt of Her severe criticism. Looking at me, Amma kept referring to the Lord as "your Kṛṣṇa!" With finality, She remarked, "Your Kṛṣṇa was a big thief. Wasn't it because of this that thieving has become universal?"

The slander was unbearable. I broke down. In between sobs, I blurted out, "My Kṛṣṇa was never the way You mentioned!"

Amma was probably waiting for this reaction, coming from deep within me, to launch a commentary on the value system established by Kṛṣṇa. As I wept like a child, unable to withstand the stinging criticism of my iṣṭa dēvata, Amma wiped away the tears streaming down my cheeks, and endearingly chided, "Are you such a small child to cry like this? Amma was only trying to gauge the depth of your bond with the Lord!"

Continuing on the subject, She explained, "Kṛṣṇa is not a thief. He is the synonym of righteousness. If He thieved at all, He did it to captivate others. When He stole butter from the *gōpīs* (cowherd women), Kṛṣṇa captured their hearts; only the Lord could do this. In this way, he succeeded in yoking the hearts of the gōpīs with the Divine, inspiring them to shift their focus from material interests to the Lord.

"When analyzed in the proper perspective, one can distinguish the underlying principle of the many things that Kṛṣṇa did—which was to turn minds inwards where one may find happiness, which had been eluding them in the outer world. An ordinary person may not realize that the Lord adopted a variety of ways to convey this message. Only when the mind is aptly and adequately tuned is it possible for one to begin comprehending the import of the Lord's actions."

The words and deeds of great Masters might be beyond our understanding, but they are always right. Only their wisdom can be a yardstick for measuring their own words and deeds. Nothing else can gauge them adequately.

Towards the end of the Kṛṣṇa Bhāva, after She had given darśan to the last devotee in the queue, Amma walked to the threshold of the kaḷari, and stood watching the devotees as they sang in blissful abandon. Savoring the soulful music, She then stepped out of the kaḷari and started dancing. This was the grand finale to the Kṛṣṇa Bhāva darśan, a flowing nṛtta that seemed to bring time to a standstill.

Nṛtta, an art form involving bodily movements choreographed to music, gives ornate expression to thoughts and feelings. It calls for a high level of concentration, and a meditative awareness that creates a divine ambience, which in turn inspires viewers to become absorbed in the dance. This identification of spectator with spectacle leads to a blissful sense of oneness.

Amma, clad in a simple costume, moved with delicate footsteps, Her hands held aloft, thumbs and forefingers held in jñānamudrā. The soul-stirring bhajans heightened the spiritual fervor, the pitch soon building up into a crescendo, inspiring the devout to sing and move with abandon, as if in a delirium.

Amma's vibrant and indefatigable dance could draw in devotees of varying spiritual caliber, uniting them in harmony and elevating them to feel a oneness with the Divine. Her feet and hands moved gracefully, Her eyes and brows communicated in the language of love and compassion, and Her smile completed this portrait of divinity as a young woman.

Amma gyrated gently to the music, entrancing the devotees who were savoring every moment of the soulful dance. Each one was a gōpa or gōpī, caught in a web of Love for their very own Amṛta Kṛṣṇa.

Amma's nṛtta was purely spiritual. It forged a bond with Her awe-struck devotees, rendered motionless by the holy vibrations overwhelming them. The coming together of the Master and Her ardent devotees generated an uplifting ambience, inducing the ecstasy of supreme love. The phenomenon was quite literally a demonstration of the dictum "*Tanmayobhavēt*" (2.2.4)—'to become one with that' (*Muṇḍakōpaniṣad*). Thus was the objective of nṛtta fulfilled.

I have had the opportunity to see quite a few classical and folk dance performances before and since, but Amma's dance was in a league of its own; this was nṛtta in its most sublime form, a līlā enacted for the single purpose of upholding dharma. Herein lies the difference between the actions of an ordinary mortal and those of mahātmas. The deeds of an enlightened Master are always aimed at uplifting or helping others, whereas our karmas arise largely from helplessness!

As the devotee crowd reveled in the Amṛta Kṛṣṇa dance that evening, the soulful nṛtta transporting them to Vṛndāvan, I found myself rendered speechless by this delectable treat. When I recall those moments, a line from the poem beginning with '*Nandakumāra Vanditarūpa*,' which I wrote some time later, comes to mind: '*Janmajarāmṛti sankaṭa-varjita santatasukhakara śaurē*'—'The valorous one who is devoid of birth, old age, death and sorrow, and who bestows everlasting happiness' is a description of the glory of Lord Kṛṣṇa.

Continuing Her dance, Amma moved into the kaḷari, and the doors closed behind Her. Thus ended the Amṛta Kṛṣṇa phase.

na tē nāmagōtrē na tē janmamṛtyū
na tē dhāmacēṣṭē na tē dukhasaukhyē
na tē mitraśatrū na tē bandhamōkṣau
tvamēkā parabrahmarūpēṇa siddhā

You have no name or lineage, birth or death, dwelling or action, pain or pleasure, friend or foe, bondage or liberation. It is evident that You exist as the one, non-dual *Parabrahma*, the Supreme!

(*Mahākālasamhita*)

Part Three

Approbation

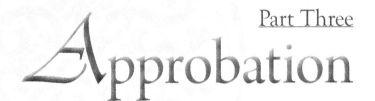

19

Sacred Silence

It was around 11 p.m. Amma emerged from the kaḷari in white robes, and walked across to the room in the adjacent house belonging to Her father Suguṇan-acchan.[26]

A small building belonging to Amma's father was being used as the residence by the family. This house was known as 'Iṭamaṇṇēl.' The room in the South, which was parallel to the lie of the kaḷari by its side, was hitherto being used by Amma to meet devotees. A narrow alley separated the room and the kaḷari. In due course of time, Suguṇan-acchan tendered the house to the āśram, and moved away to another

26 Amma's father's name is Suguṇānandan, and 'acchan' ('father'), indicates the respect being accorded.

dwelling in the neighborhood. Amma has endearingly referred to Suguṇan-acchan as the āśram's '*kāvalbhaṭan,*' its sentinel. The āśram has developed into a huge institution, but we should never forget its humble beginnings, especially the sacrifice and renunciation that Suguṇan-acchan, Damayanti-amma and their family members underwent. Words can never suffice to describe adequately their role in the growth of the āśram.

A little over half an hour had elapsed, and with the brief session with the visitors over, Amma was seen walking back to the kaḷari, the mood and the expectancy of the on-looking devotees heralding the awesome spectacle of Dēvī Bhāva[27] that would unfold soon.

The air was getting charged, with devotees shuffling about to get a glimpse of Amma as She walked back into the kaḷari. Piety marked the mood all around, an indication of the spiritual grandeur of the event about to be unveiled. The tintinnabulation of the bronze bells fused with the heralding notes of the conch. It sent resonant waves of hope, relief and reassurance—rising over the devotees, and fanning out into the abundant mesh of trees made denser by the thick growth of shrubs—to merge with the roaring waves of the ocean in the background.

27 In narrating this phase of the evening program, recourse has been taken to address it endearingly as Dēvī Manifestation, Dēvī Form and Amṛtā Dēvī.

The doors to the shrine closed. Amma was changing into the Dēvī garb. Time lingered as the devotees, charged with spiritual fervor, waited with bated breath for Amma to reappear. There was pin-drop silence.

There is silence, and there is silence. In the first instance, silence is a natural corollary to deep wisdom. In the second, silence is the wisest recourse for the ignorant, especially in the company of the wise. Only then can one imbibe their knowledge.

Mother worship is a distinct philosophy in itself, which holds that Śakti or Dēvī (the Divine Mother) is the absolute, ultimate Godhead. Śakti is the impartial energy of the universe manifesting as unconditional love. Like the sun that shines on the good and bad alike, the mother stands by her child through thick and thin, giving credence to the pre-eminence of the mother principle.

Since Vēdic times, worship of the Divine has found diverse expressions, depending on the devotional moods, one of the most heart-warming being that of a child towards its mother. Ṛg-Vēdic pronouncements such as "*Mātēva yadbharasē paprathānō janañjanam*" (5.15.4) ("Agni who sustains all beings like the mother") and "*Vayam syāma māturna sūnavaḥ*" (7.81.4) ("Let us be dear to you, like sons to a mother") are testimony to the eminence of this devotional attitude.

The '*kalaśa*' (pitcher or pot) is traditionally regarded as the symbol of the womb, '*garbha*,' for it sustains human life. The '*pūrṇakalaśa*,' considered a sign of abundance and the source of life, is a Vēdic motif known from the earliest of times. The pot, ever revered as a symbol of divinity, was equated with the mother. Our concept of the universe existing in a cosmic womb is analogous to the principle of deities enshrined in the *garbha gṛha* (sanctum sanctorum) of temples. The *Ṛg-Vēda* proclaims:

> *Hiraṇyagarbhaḥ samavartatāgrē bhūtasya jātaḥ patirēka āsīt*
>
> In the beginning was Hiraṇyagarbha, the Lord of all beings. *(10.121.1)*

In the *Durgā Sūktam*, a strikingly beautiful Vēdic hymn, the Divine Mother has been extolled thus:

> *Tāmagnivarṇām tapasā jvalantīm vairōcanīm karmaphalēṣu juṣṭām*
>
> *Durgām dēvīm śaraṇamaham prapadyē sutarasi tarasē namaḥ*
>
> I take refuge in Goddess Durgā, glowing like fire with the power of Her penance, and established in

> the form of the fruits of actions. Salutation to Thee, who steers us expertly across the sea of grief.
>
> *(Taittirīyāraṇyakam, 4.10.2)*

In this sacred land of Bhāratam, God has been looked upon as the feminine par excellence, and women, as manifestations of the Divine Mother. She is not only the Mother of the universe; She is also the Eternal Virgin.

Amma is addressed as 'Amma' or 'Ammachi' by Her devotees all over the world. 'Amma' is the word for 'mother' in many regions of South India. However, while referring to Amma, 'Ammachi,' the colloquial form usually used in various parts of Kēraḷa, has become current among many devotees, including foreigners. Once, giving an indication of Her divine origin, Amma said, "I am Amma as well as '*Machi*,'"[28] driving home the point that the Universal Mother is both the Mother of all the created worlds as well as the Eternal Virgin. She added, "I am the origin and hence related to all, yet I am free and detached from everyone."

---

28 A colloquial term to describe a woman who has never given birth; ('Amma' + 'Machi' = 'Ammachi').

20

Queenly Qualm

Śrī Śankara's *Mātṛpañcakam* pays tribute to the unfathomable dimensions of a mother's unselfish love:

> *Yasyā kṣamō dātum niṣkṛtimunnatōSpi tanayastasyai jananyai namaḥ*
>
> I prostrate to that mother to whom no son, however eminent he may be, can ever hope to repay the debt due to her (for the endless suffering and sacrifices she has undergone for the child's sake). (1)

The mother principle is invaluable in creation. It refers to all that gives life, and is thus a synonym for nature. A mother helps to create a prosperous and blissful world for her children. She helps them adapt to the vagaries of nature, and also teaches them how to surmount the obstacles one may confront in life. The abundant love flowing out of her maternal heart is the mainstay supporting them on their voyage to success.

There is a popular story from Rājasthāni folklore about a queen who took great pains to bring up her young son to become a worthy prince who would eventually take over the reins as royal head. Once, when the grown-up prince was on a tour of the villages bordering his state, a messenger brought him news about a stream of refugees from the neighboring state, now in siege, trying to cross into their kingdom to beg for asylum. The prince rode out to meet the refugees in an open ground.

The immigrants poured out their tale of woe. Forced to flee from their homes, they had been left destitute and homeless. They implored the prince's help so that they could earn a livelihood. The prince was moved by the heart-rending plight of the refugees, and genuinely wanted to help them. He told them that he would convey their request to the queen and return the next day.

When the prince returned to the state capital, he apprised the queen about the refugees and requested her to grant him permission to rehabilitate them. The queen looked stunned, and then exclaimed, "How and where did I err in your upbringing and the inculcation of righteous royal values?"

The prince did not understand what his mother meant. The queen immediately sent for the chief maid-in-waiting.

When she arrived, the queen asked her, "Tell me, when and why my instruction to ensure that the prince was to be fed only my breast milk was ignored?"

Gauging the gravity in the queen's tone, the chief maid blurted out the truth. She said, "Forgive me, your Highness! On one occasion when the child was six months old, when you had to leave in an emergency to visit a distant post, and returned only late in the night, the young child cried and cried out of hunger until I could stand it no more, and I breastfed the baby myself."

The queen now turning to her son said, "I was wondering why you had to come all the way here for my counsel, leaving the hapless refugees in the cold to starve and suffer further for a day and night! With the upbringing intended to be given to you, the decision should have occurred to you on the spot!"

21

Broken Bond

Although my birth mother had passed away even before I could toddle, the ethics she espoused continued to sustain and reinforce the value system already in the family. Growing up, I could feel the magnitude of her contribution to my spiritual inclinations.

Her name would often be mentioned as an example of meticulous conduct and rigorous dedication to religious and spiritual practices. An episode that took place during her last days provides a glimpse into her pious nature.

An ardent Kṛṣṇa devotee, my mother breathed her last after a terminal disease for which medical science did not have a cure. The story of the last minutes of her life created an indelible impression on my young mind.

Shortly before she passed away, my mother had said that she was not going to live for much longer, and then asked for a knife so that she could sever the necklace with the '*tāli*';[29] the act was symbolic of cutting off all ties to temporal

29 The word 'tāli,' used in many parts of South India, refers to a necklace or pendant that the bridegroom ties around the bride's neck during the marriage rites.

life. As the family members around her were figuring out what she was trying to say, she almost immediately called out loudly, as if to an unseen presence, "I asked for a knife to cut this tāli. Are you giving me the '*Sudarśana cakra*'[30] instead?"

In Hindu culture, the 'tāli' symbolizes the inseparable bond between the husband and wife. It is more commonly referred to as '*Māngalyasūtram*.' During the wedding ceremony, the bridegroom ties the māngalyasūtram around the bride's neck, uttering, "May you live long by wearing this Māngalyasūtram." Married women wear the mangaḷasūtra throughout their married life. It is believed that doing so augurs well for the husband and hence the family. It is also said that the mangaḷasūtra protects the marriage from evil influences.

The *Śrī Laḷitā Sahasranāma* attribute to Dēvī—"*Kāmēśabaddha māngalyasūtra śōbhitakandharā*" (30) ("The Goddess whose neck is adorned by the māngaḷyasūtram tied by Kāmēśa (Lord Śiva) Her divine consort)"—points to the rich significance of the tāli and the ancient roots of this tradition.

Under normal circumstances, a person in the last stage of life generally asks to see his or her near and dear ones, the strength of earthly ties proving greater than any desire

30 The divine disk (weapon) associated with Lord Viṣṇu.

for freedom from bondage. Rarely does a departing soul embrace the impending journey with ease. This requires extensive preparation. If the cultural and religious milieu one is born into is conducive to spiritual progress, part of the task is done. If one's own efforts are added to enhance the readiness to relinquish all ties, then the blessed soul will be able to shuffle off his mortal coil with ease. The key is yearning for God.

The instance, where my late mother asked for a knife to cut the Māngalyasūtra, is referred to in great awe, even today, by people who knew her. The mention of the Sudarśana Cakra, the iconic weapon associated with Lord Kṛṣṇa, her personal deity, indicated the depth of the deity-devotee bond. That she breathed her last, chanting "*Kṛṣṇā! Kṛṣṇā!*" underscored her intense affinity to the Lord.

I often wonder if it is not because of this deep vein of devotion that runs through generations in our family that Amma came to the taravāṭ at Māvēlikkara countless times. When Amma visited our home for the first time, She gazed at the portrait of my mother for several minutes. She told me that the departed soul had come home to Her heart. Amma's words were, for me, a reassurance that my mother had, in her short but immensely soulful life dedicated to religious and spiritual activities, merged into Her deity's lotus feet.

According to the scriptures, a person's next birth is determined largely by the predominant thought(s) prevailing at the time of the soul's departure. If this be the case, then my mother, chanting the Lord's name as she passed away, had certainly attained the Lord's abode. Amma, the omniscient one, must have perceived this as She stood looking intently at my mother's portrait, Her hands spontaneously forming *mudrās*.'[31]

> *Antakālē ca māmēva smaran muktvā kaḷēbaram*
> *yaḥ prayāti sa madbhāvam yāti nāstyatra samśayaḥ*
> Whoever gives up his body remembering Me alone at the time of death becomes one with Me; there is no doubt about it. (*Bhagavad Gītā*, 8.5)

If one hopes to remember God at the time of death also, one should practice remembering Him throughout life.

As Amma turned away from the portrait, She asked me, "Do you fret over the absence of your mother?" Placing Her hand over Her heart, Amma then said, "She is here right now. Your mother was born to deliver both of you into this world."

---

31 Gesture; in this context, a mystic gesture.

22

Glorious Goddess

The doors finally opened, and Amma came into view wearing a long skirt and blouse, the sleeves extending almost to Her elbow and the skirt reaching down to Her ankles and feet. The long, curly, luxuriant cascade of hair flowing down Her back resembled the tumultuous gush of the celestial Ganges.

Sporting overlapping vermilion and sandal-paste marks on the sky of Her brows, Amma's visage was a study in tranquility. Modest ornaments—a few bangles and rings—enhanced the shapeliness of Her slender hands and tapering fingers. An alluring aura added splendor to Her majestic form. Taking the ārati lamp, Amma started to perform ārati to the decorated pedestal meant for seating Dēvī. Waving the camphor flame in a sweeping, clockwise motion, Amma concluded the brief worship of the bedecked platform.

The ārati over, Amma sat down in front of the consecrated pedestal and started crooning a devotional song in Her impassioned and melodious voice, its charismatic strains flowing out into and permeating the enveloping darkness outside. The flow was often broken by ecstatic exclamations suggestive of an inner jubilation. At the height of this rapture, Amma started as if springing out from Her seat, swaying back and forth in rhythm with the hymn She was singing. The general ambience was suggestive of the overflow of cosmic energy that subtly characterized Amṛtā Dēvī.

The air was saturated by the Spirit animating the following lines of '*Durgā Saptaśatī*' (a book highlighting the epic glory of the Universal Mother Durgā):

Hinasti daityatējāmsī svanēnāpūrya yā jagat
Sā ghaṇṭā pātu no dēvi pāpēbhyōSnaḥ sutāniva

O Goddess, You annihilate the powers of the demons with Your voice, ringing like the bell that pervades the whole universe. May the sound of that bell protect us from our sins like the mother protecting her children. (11.27)

The doors to the kaḷari closed once again. One could then hear from the closed sanctum sanctorum shrill calls of ecstasy, charging the hitherto serene environment with an air of hushed expectancy. Amma's unearthly calls, daunting as they were, inspired awe, reverence and devotion in the hearts of all.

This was the signal for Suguṇan-acchan, Amma's father, to embark on the ceremonial cleansing that is part of Dēvī worship. He had a small urn filled with holy water and, circumambulating the kaḷari, would sprinkle it along the path and on the devotees assembled there, invoking sanctity all around. (Traditionally, the sprinkling of holy water signifies the purification of the external environment.)

Manu's[32] code of conduct for society laid immense stress on the reverence to be accorded to women, highlighting the significance of the Mother principle. The following verse reveals the singular importance given in traditional society to women: "*Yatra nāryastu pūjyantē ramantē tatra dēvatāḥ*" (*Manusmṛti*, 3.56)—"Where women are worshipped, there the gods dwell in joy."

In the Purāṇic tale, *Tripurārahasyam*, there is a dialogue between the two principal characters, Hēmacūḍa and Hēmalēkha, which reveals the supremacy of Goddess Tripurasundarī. Profoundly inspired by his consort's narration, Hēmacūḍa asks, "From the pantheon of gods and goddesses, replete with a wide range of names and forms and associated

32 Progenitor of humanity.

attributes, whom should I chose for my spiritual elevation and eventual liberation?"

The wise and evolved Hēmalēkha replies, "Truth is one; the wise call it by various names. God has neither name nor form, nor limiting adjuncts like time and space. He is not Brahmā or Viṣṇu or Śiva. However, since it is difficult to apprehend the Impersonal God (without attributes), human beings worship Him as a Personal God with names and forms. How is it possible for the limited human mind to comprehend the myriad manifestations of the infinite Godhead? The devotee can choose any form he likes. What is important is pure devotion and sincerity, not the form one chooses. Where there is devotion and sincerity, God will respond by assuming a form that corresponds to the devotee's imaginative resolve; that devotee will eventually attain the Supreme Abode. The Lord is ever fond of and compassionate to His devotees. He is pure consciousness. This omnipotent and omniscient consciousness shines as Mahādēvī, the Supreme Goddess, Tripurasundarī, in whom the whole cosmos abides. So, whatever form one worships, one is, in effect, worshipping the Divine Mother."

No matter which path he pursues, the seeker will undoubtedly evolve if he is sincere. The *Yōgavāsiṣṭham* hints at what awaits a progressing aspirant:

Yāvadyāvad paralōkaḥ paramātmaiva śiṣyatē

Tāvattāvanmahābāhō svayam samtyajyatēSkhilam
O mighty warrior! As it becomes more and more clear with intense contemplation that the supreme Self alone exists, the entire world of plurality will disappear by itself.

In the first chapter of the *Durgā Saptaśatī*, there is a section where Lord Brahmā praises Dēvī. The following lines delineate the cosmic dimensions of the Divine Mother:

Visṛṣṭau sṛṣṭirūpā tvam sthitirūpā ca pālanē
tathā samhṛtirūpāntē jagatōSsya jaganmayē
O Mother of the Universe, You are the Creator at the time of creation, Sustainer at the time of sustaining, and in the end, Destroyer at the time of the dissolution of the universe. (1.76 - 77)

Śāktēyam is a denomination of the traditional school of Dēvī worship, which regards Śakti or Dēvī (the Divine Mother) as the absolute, ultimate Godhead. This, along with Śaivism and Vaiṣṇavism,[33] constitute the three primary schools of worship. Śāktēyam regards Dēvī as the Supreme Consciousness itself, 'one without a second,' all other forms

33 *Śāktēyam—Doctrine of power, or doctrine of the Goddess; Śaivism—Doctrine pertaining to Śiva; Vaiṣṇavism—Doctrine pertaining to Viṣṇu.*

of divinity, female or male, considered merely Her diverse manifestations!

An outstanding commentary on the diverse and divine dimensions of the Universal Mother is found in the Ṛg-Vēdic '*Dēvī Sūktam*' (10.125). The hymn is a rhapsodic expression of the state of realization by 'Vāk,'[34] daughter of Sage Ambhrina, who sings a paean to the all-encompassing nature of the Mother thus:

> I (Brahman) move in the form of the Rudras, Vasus, Ādityas and all other gods. The sovereign power am I, as also bestower of all wealth, and the first to whom sacrificial homage is to be offered. All gods worship Me in all my diversity of forms. I permeate everything. The infinite expanse above the earth is my offspring. I am born deep in the sea, from where I permeate all the worlds, touching the empyrean with My body. Blowing like the wind, I create the whole universe. I am beyond heaven and earth. Such is My magnitude.

34 The Sānskṛt word for speech, voice or language, from the root 'vac,' meaning speak, tell or utter. Personified, Vāk is a Goddess. Most frequently, She is identified with Saraswatī (also known as Bhāratī), Goddess of Speech. In scriptural texts, She is called the Mother of the Vēdas, among other attributes.

23

Fragrant Fusion

There is a moving story in the *Tiruviḷayāṭal Purāṇam*[35] about a herd of piglets who were orphaned and left to fend for themselves in the forest, crying for their mother's milk. Once, a *Pāṇḍya* king of Madurai went to hunt in the forest. Sighting a group of wild boar, he decided to hunt them for game. Seeing the king coming towards them, the leader of the herd began conferring with his wife. Knowing the king's prowess in hunting, she counseled her companion to scoot away to safety. The boar scoffed at the suggestion on the ground that it was not in keeping with the valor and spirit of their clan, citing the proverb: "You might see a boar standing between two lions and drinking water from a river, but you will never see a lion daring to stand between two boars to drink water!"

Saying thus, he charged at the king's men, killing and wounding many, but finally was killed by the king. The mother boar, watching the turn of events, jumped into the

35 A compendium (in Tamil) of 64 tales of Lord Śiva in and around the Mīnākṣī temple shrine in Madurai.

fray and fought valiantly but was soon lanced by a soldier. The piglets were left behind. Soon, with the heat of the sun and pangs of hunger and thirst tormenting them, they started wailing.

Lord Śiva and Mother Pārvatī, who were disguised as birds and perched on a nearby tree, noticed the plight of the piglets. The Mother, compassion personified, requested Her consort to relieve the piglets of their misery, whereupon the Lord assumed the form of their slain mother and breastfed them to health and well-being. In doing so, the Lord highlighted the vital significance of the Mother.

One might well ask, why couldn't Pārvatī have assumed the form of the slain mother boar and breastfed the piglets Herself? The answer could be that this story is an allegory that shows how motherhood is not restricted to women only. Lord Śiva responded immediately to Pārvatī's request, expressing His own motherly compassion as breast milk. In Śiva and Pārvatī, we find a perfect blend of the feminine and masculine.

Generally, women are regarded as predominantly emotional, and men, as largely rational. Some hold that the twain can never meet. But as the parable above illustrates, they can. In fact, the very purpose of marriage can be seen as bringing about a blend of the two. A harmonious balance of these traits can ensure a successful married life.

The love and compassion of the Mother in the Goddess takes the form of an appeal to Her consort. The latter responds without any chauvinistic sentiment such as "Why can't you breastfeed the piglets yourself? After all, you're the woman!" Instead, He summons the pure emotion of motherhood.

Equally significant is the fact that it took Pārvatī, a woman, to elicit this pure emotion in man. In the final analysis, the qualities of love and compassion are necessary for male and female alike.

To quote Amma, paragon of love and concern, "A person who has no compassion for the suffering of others isn't spiritual at all. Such a person will never see God." Indeed, of what worth is spiritual striving if one's heart remains unmoved by suffering?

The doors of the kaḷari finally opened. Amma came into view, striding forward with a sword in the right hand and a trident in the left. She stopped just outside the kaḷari, turned to face South, and started dancing with unusually long and graceful strides, moving smoothly in front of the shrine, the body gliding effortlessly as She brandished the sword and the trident with swift flourishes.

The rhythm from the *tabla* and other percussion instruments matched Amma's footsteps splendidly. Accompanied by other musical instruments, the bhajan group sat facing the North, providing robust support to the dance. The heady blend—rousing singing, scintillating beats and meaningful lyrics, on the one hand, and the soul-stirring sight of Amma's dance, on the other—created an indelible impression in the minds of those present, fostering a deep immersion into the meditative ambience.

Where Amṛta Kṛṣṇa transmitted a mood of overwhelming joy, a state of pure Bliss, Amṛtā Dēvī inspired devotion, reverence, love and compassion, inducing a deep awe in everyone. Bliss is the outcome of spiritual practices. Many not only are unaware of this, they cannot understand and recognize this happiness even when they see those in bliss. As Emerson famously remarked, "Life is a festival only to the wise."

I thought that Amma would continue Her nṛtta-līlā in front of the kaḷari, but She broke away from the scene and ran outside into the open. As Amma moved around, Her form keenly watched by devotees, She would flourish the sword freely and gracefully in the air, as if driving out the evil forces lurking in the outer darkness and dispelling the inner darkness from the hearts of Her children. The lights in the kaḷari and its surroundings were just about adequate to illuminate the immediate area, while the outlying areas were cloaked in the darkness of the night.

Amma danced away in large strides into the darkness outside. She would disappear for some time, making Her presence in the far distance felt only by the tinkling sounds of Her anklets and the powerful shouts She let out in Her supercharged state. She strode here and there, homing in on different spots from various directions, traversing wildly in the pitch dark.

Truly, the ways of the Goddess are incomprehensible; without Her grace, She is hard to attain, too. 'Dēvī' is synonymous with 'Durgā,' which means: "*Duḥkhēna gantum śakyā*" ("one who can be realized only through intense struggle or severe penance").

Subsequently, I learned that at this time, Amma would circumambulate those spiritual aspirants who had come to be present at the Dēvī Bhāva darśan and were sitting in deep meditation in solitary locations in and around the place. As Amma revealed later, She intentionally undertook such forays to prevent evil forces from causing impediments to these seekers of Truth.

Dēvī has been glorified in *Viśvasāratantra* thus: "*Namastē jagaccintyamānasvarūpē*" ("I bow to Thee (O Divine Mother), whose true form is the object of meditation for the whole world").

Amma's captivating dance covered all the areas outside the kaḷari. She then walked majestically towards the devotees who had gathered in front of the kaḷari in a large circular formation. Amma slowly walked by the devotees, allowing them to prostrate before Her and touch Her holy feet. "All is holy where devotion kneels." (O.W. Holmes[36])

The intense devotion with which devotees swarmed like bees around Amma that evening has not diminished over the years. It continues, day in and day out, as devotees throng to Amma wherever She may be, craving to touch Her feet and remain attached in the magnetic presence of this Master. Their faith arises from Her ocean of love and compassion, which is not limited to the immediate ring of devotees but reaches out to all sentient and insentient beings in nature.

After Her brief interaction with the devotees gathered around the kaḷari, Amma moved back to the front of the kaḷari and commenced dancing once again, captivating one and all with Her briskness and brio as She moved in graceful circles, incandescent with energy. The music of the bhajans, its pulse and flow, superbly supported the dance of Kāḷī.

36 Oliver Wendell Holmes, Sr. (1809 – 1894), an American physician, poet, professor and author.

24

Providential Pull

The significance of Dēvī *upāsana* (worship) on the psyche of devotees was made amply clear by the impact Amma's Dēvī Manifestation had on them. At the end of the entrancing nṛtta, Amma went inside the kaḷari shrine, the doors closing behind Her. When the doors opened again after a brief spell, the devotees saw the splendid sight of Amma wearing a crown and silk sāri, seated majestically. Amma's benign countenance expressed indescribable compassion, inspiring fresh new waves of devotion in the hearts of devotees. The ringing of bells, the rousing blow of the conch, the rhythmic beats of drums, and lilting notes of the bhajan melded to create a soundscape that seemed to echo the joy and fervor the devotees felt as ārati was performed to Amma in Dēvī Form.

As the ārati flame was being waved in wide circular motions, Amma sat with eyes closed, Her demeanor a study in meditative repose. The thrill of beholding divinity in flesh and blood was expressed in the music and in the body language of the devotees; the very ambience seemed charged with a mystic air. The devotional fervor of the devotees expressed itself in ecstatic cries: "*Ammē, Dēvī!*" "*Ammachi!*" "*Dēvi Ammachi!*"

There is an anecdote about E.I. Bosworth, a theologian, who was asked, "How do you know there is God?" In response, he narrated the instance of the time he had encountered a small boy flying a kite. The kite, which was flying so high that it was literally out of sight, prompted him to ask the boy, "How do you know there is any kite there at all?"

The boy replied, "I feel the pull of it!"

The devotees in and around the kaḷari could feel the tug of the divine. As soon as the ārati was over, they began queuing up for darśan. I joined them instinctively, my mind earnestly looking for a repeat of the soulful experience I had enjoyed during the Kṛṣṇa Bhāva darśan earlier.

While awaiting my turn for darśan, I noticed Amma reaching out once in a while to a small bottle containing a red-colored liquid. I learned later that it was a brew prepared from red hibiscus flowers and lime juice. Small doses of this concoction used to be given to devotees seeking medical relief. There was another vessel with a long snout filled with holy water that Amma would give the devotees. To those seeking respite from various kinds of physical afflictions, Amma would also prescribe turmeric.

> *Rōgānaśēṣānapahamsi tuṣṭā*
> O Dēvi! When You are pleased, You cause all afflictions to cease!
> *(Durgā Saptaśatī, 11.29)*

My turn for darśan came and, with utmost reverence, I touched Amma's feet. Giving me Her characteristic hug, She gently laid me on Her lap with the care lavished on newborns, stroking my back gently for a while. I felt as if the Universal Mother was giving me relief from the mental agony gnawing my insides. Lifting me up and clasping me in Her motherly embrace, Amma soothed my agitations as She softly and sweetly intoned, "*mōnē*," "*mōne*" ("dear son") into my ears. The experience was beyond words. I yielded to the overwhelming flow of pure maternal love that liberated me from all anxieties, uncertainties and nagging worries.

In hindsight, I saw that darśan as an endearing attempt on the part of an indulgent mother to allay the anxieties of a son caught in a quagmire of indecision. When I realized how much Amma was trying to calm me, I felt a surge of immense gratitude welling up in my heart for Her infinite mercy and grace.

Amma motioned me to sit by Her side. I was conscious of Amma watching me as She glanced sideways once in a while. I could discern a gamut of moods in Amma, evoking fear, devotion, chaste affection, as well as pure and innocent love.

I was in for a major surprise. Some time later, Amma handed me Her sword and asked me to meditate. Rare is the opportunity for anyone to be directed to sit close to Amma, and even rarer is the instance when a devotee is given the sword to hold and meditate in Her proximity. I was dazed for a moment by this special treatment. I felt deeply humbled by Amma's benevolence and grace.

Owing to the accumulated fatigue from the traveling and hours of waiting, as well as the late hour (it was past midnight), I fell asleep. Holding me by my chin, Amma gently drew my head to Her lap, and caressed my back with Her hand, as my head tossed gently with the throbbing of Her leg. (In the early days of Kṛṣṇa and Dēvī Bhāvas, Amma's body used to vibrate continuously.)

She thus kept me *awake*, and *aware*, throughout the night. This experience, dovetailing with my earlier experience with Amma at my aunt's house, left me wondering if this was not part of a pre-ordained script from the larger play She was enacting in Her current incarnation!

Later, as darśan progressed, I watched with awe the manner in which Amma held each devotee in Her arms, and Her lively, sensitive and reassuring interactions with them. But what took my breath away was how Amma showered Her love and compassion on Dattan, a devotee seriously afflicted by leprosy. The sight of his body, with its open and oozing sores, would have repulsed even the most understanding person in the world. But Amma took him lovingly into Her arms and gave him as tight a hug as She would have given to any other devotee, even though Her clothes were becoming soiled by the blood and pus issuing from the open lesions on the devotee's face, hands and body. What astounded me further was the way Amma held him with both Her hands and started licking the open sores on his face and body. Her saliva had a beneficial effect on his terrible affliction. Amma kept up this treatment for the next few years until Dattan was totally healed.

An eloquent attribute addressed to Rudra, the principal deity in the worship of '*Rudram*' is, "*Prathamō daivyō bhiṣak*" (1.6), hailing the primordial Lord Rudra as the first and foremost divine physician. Based on what I had observed, I could only hail Amma as "the great, consummate doctor."

"The saliva of an evolved soul bears immense spiritual potency," was how Amma would explain this mode of relief to us in later times. Here, Amma's spiritual resolve manifested in Her saliva to medicate and relieve the suffering devotee.

A reputed doctor, who is an ardent devotee of Amma, would go off frequently to meet Her, arousing the curiosity of his colleagues. When they asked him where he was going to so often, he would reply, "I'm going to see *my* doctor!"

I stood watching Amma in wonderment, Her eyes radiating love and compassion. Her pose suggested valor, indicating a determination to remove the impediments to the peace and well-being of Her devotees. In a flash, I perceived Her as the Universal Mother.

At the end of the Dēvī Bhāva, Amma showered flowers at the devotees while standing inside the kaḷari. A few minutes later, the doors to the shrine closed. It was past four in the morning.

There was no mistaking the cosmic pre-eminence of this Master. I could see both the light at the end of the tunnel in the search for my bearings as well as the beacon that could guide me on the intended path. There was nothing more left for me to deliberate upon as I consciously and spontaneously made my decision.

25

Total Transformation

My aunt and I left the āśram before five in the morning. Despite the darkness obscuring the trail outside, the inner sun shone and appeared to pick out the path for me, distinguishing it from all others, like a road highlighted in a map. For the first time in my life, I knew where to go and how to get there.

My aunt and I reached Kayamkuḷam at around 6:30 a.m. While waiting for the early bus to Māvēlikkara, I noticed people moving about, the eastern sky gradually brightening, ushering in the golden rays of the early morning sun, and erasing all signs of the preceding darkness. Suddenly, aware of the sea change within me, I found myself surprised by the mundane purposes stirring those people to action. Previously, I would have taken such phenomena for granted as an innocuous feature of the daily rat race. But now, having derived immense bliss from the interactions with Amma, I was amused to no end by the sight of these people scurrying about their daily chores. I found it rather odd that the people here could be so oblivious to the resplendent light in the form of Amma, available at their doorstep to show them the way. Instead, as if possessed by the sight of a beckoning mirage, they were enamored of their life pursuits! I realized that the maze of material charms was luring them to decided bondage. This was a new understanding for me. How extremely blessed I was to have acquired what they lacked.

As the bus drew up to my destination in Māvēlikkara, I was shaken out of my reverie. Now that my goal was defined, I had a small job left to do. I told my aunt to go ahead, and that I would see her at home a little later. I then went into a barber's salon to have my head shaved. The thick growth of healthy, black hair—the envy of all my college-mates, the object of appreciation and, very often, admiration by girls of the college—had to go. The pains I had taken to preserve its gloss and growth were, in a moment of realization, being recognized for their futility, highlighting the impermanence of material possessions.

There had been occasions when my father would insist on my having a haircut, and I would find some excuse or the other to avoid it. One of my professors had also pointedly asked me take a look in the mirror, suggesting indirectly the dire need for a haircut. Girls would flatter me by jokingly staking a claim to the cut hair, should I decide to trim it! On looking back, it is easy to see the misplaced pride material attractions offered. The great Master had transformed me in a few hours. That morning, asking the barber to shear my prized locks from their roots came so easily to me. In retrospect, it is clear that such an instantly radical transformation has to be attributed to Amma's immense power. Only someone rooted in the ultimate spiritual experience can bring about such a transformation; otherwise it is impossible, even if oceans of ink are spilled in explicating the Truth. Books or intellectuals may bring about a temporary conviction, but only a realized Master can bring forth a deep-rooted change.

Amma has said, "Children, you have all been with Amma in many past lives. That is why you are here with Amma now." The spiritual merit I might have gained from those lives spent with Amma is the only explanation I can think of for the transformation that came over me literally overnight! *Sannyāsōpaniṣad* hints at the relevance of virtuous acts and the positive effects accruing from previous births: "*Prākpuṇyakarmaviśēṣāt*" (1.19) ("By virtue of meritorious deeds done in previous births").

In the *Mahābhārata*, there is an instance when Bhīṣma comments on the unerring manifestation of the fruits of karma, comparing it with the calf's natural instinct in finding the trail of its mother cow through a herd of grazing cattle. He recounts the conversation between Prahḷāda and the evolved soul Ajagara. Prahḷāda asks, "What is that trait in a human being that stands to liberate him from sorrows in life? What should he do to gain spiritual transcendence?"

Ajagara replies, "The perplexing births in the created world, its highs and lows are all entirely dependent on the results of one's karma. All are slaves to their own nature; what more is left for one to understand, who perceives the cycle of births and deaths? Regulated by time, death occurs; it encompasses every created being in its fold!" He then adds, "One who manages to overcome his own nature can freely exist anywhere; nothing will affect him!" Death is the only certainty, and God is the only Truth.

The scriptures declare:

> *Viṣayēṣvaniśam rāgō manasō malamucyatē*
> *tēṣvēva vītarāgatvam nirmalatvamudāhṛtam*
>
> Attachment to sense objects is called impurity of the mind. On the contrary, detachment from them is described as purity of the mind.

Once, during my early years in the āśram, I asked Amma a question that sprouted from the genuine curiosity of the seeker in me. "What is the sign of spiritual progress in a *sādhak* (aspirant)?"

Amma's response was spontaneous and brief: "His personal character, my son!"

I recalled the story of the king who was deeply attached to his lovely wife. She was singularly beautiful. The king doted on her, showering her with priceless gifts. Unusually wise and a model of perfection in both her personal capacity and as royal companion, the queen was an invaluable asset to the king. Their connubial bliss proved to be short-lived. The queen died, depriving the uxorious king of her joyous company.

There was no end to the king's distress. He was so attached to his wife's beauty that he would not permit the disposal of the dead body. Instead, he ordered the best and most beautiful mausoleum to be built for the dead queen. After the king approved the proposed plan, construction began, drawing the most skilled laborers from all over the country and the rarest resources from remote locations. Months later, the edifice was ready. When the time came for the burial, the king ordered the coffin to be brought to him so that he could take one last look. The sarcophagus was brought and the lid was lifted up for the king to see his dearest, the departed queen, for the last time. When the king saw the partially decayed and decomposed body inside the coffin, he was aghast! It was nothing like the form he had been mentally cherishing all these months of grief. In sheer disgust, he ordered, "Take it away!"

Such is the fate of even the strongest attachment—revulsion. One should rise above both *rāga* and *dvēṣa*, attachment

and aversion. Detachment is the equilibrium attained when the pendulum of likes and dislikes ceases its oscillation.

26

Sanctum Sanctorum

After the tonsure at the hairdressing salon, I left for my aunt's house, took a bath and, smearing holy ash all over my body like yōgīs (influenced by the form of Ācārya Śankara in the movie), sped off to the taravāṭ on a bicycle. I cycled a distance of less than four kilometers, provoking bewilderment in many of the acquaintances, relatives and friends I passed. I sensed that they were silently mocking the transformation they saw, probably wondering what had happened to the level-headed youth they knew. On my part, I pitied them for the humdrum existence they were continuing to live without realizing the fruitlessness of the material life, especially since Amma was right in their midst, waiting to take them to freedom.

I reached the ancestral house. Seeing my drastically changed appearance, my elders were stunned, as if in disbelief. In spite of their visible shock, they stood up to greet me with folded palms, a subdued gesture of reverence. This show of respect, revealing an abrupt change in their attitude, added an unexpected boost to my self-esteem; it also reflected Amma's immense clout. How else could one explain the reverential conduct of these elders, who had hitherto never behaved this way to me?

An elder spoke out at last, "My dear child, what is this?"

I replied with conviction, "I do not wish to continue my present way of life. I have decided to leave for Vaḷḷikkāvu and join Amma as Her disciple."

There was an uproar, with all other family members joining in. The news, when it spread to my father's house, in Harippāṭ, triggered even more of a furor. Some of them even started putting the blame squarely on my aunt for facilitating my meeting with Amma and subsequent visit to Vaḷḷikkāvu.

To some extent, their reaction can be attributed to the mainstream belief that upon marriageable age, one should embrace a householder's life. The alternative—dedicating oneself to the spiritual path at a young age, and living a life of renunciation—was not acceptable to them, even though there is a time-honored tradition of monasticism in India. In due course, though, all of them became ardent devotees of Amma.

There was a time during my initial years in the āśram when I would ask Amma questions frequently and seek clarifications from Her. On one occasion, I asked, "Amma, what is the fundamental objective of life?"

Amma's reply was spontaneous and profoundly subtle. "Everlasting tranquility of the mind is verily the realization of the soul. Don't ever forget it," She said.

A reference in the *Chāndōgyōpaniṣad* underscores the truth that real happiness cannot be found in indulgence in material pleasures; it can be gained only from awareness of the Self. This is revealed in an interaction between Sage Uddālaka and his son Śvētakētu when the father explains thus: "Just as a bird tied to a string, after flying in various directions and finding no resting place elsewhere, takes refuge at the very place where it is tied to, even so, dear boy, that mind, after flying in various directions and finding no resting place elsewhere, takes refuge in *Prāṇa* (Soul) alone; for the mind, dear boy, is tied to Prāṇa" (6.8.2).

People at home were greatly distressed by my transformation, but even more turbulent and restless was my mind. It was obsessed with just one thought: to see Amma in Vaḷḷikkāvu. The turmoil steadily increased with every passing hour, until I could stand it no longer. In spite of the reservations of people at home, I left for my aunt's place early the next day. I told her about the restlessness of my mind and insisted on leaving for Vaḷḷikkāvu to meet Amma immediately.

Giving in to my earnest request, she set out with me for Vaḷḷikkāvu without further delay. We had to go by public bus, and the ride was going to take a few hours at least. I wondered if my restive mind could stand a journey that long. My physical system was showing all signs of distress: my parched throat thirsting for a swig of water, my increasing breathlessness craving an extra supply of oxygen, and the digestive and connected excretory faculties unsure of whether I had to answer nature's call immediately! The mind was racing ahead to Amma, but the body was unable to keep pace with it, and was reacting terribly!

Eons after I boarded it, the bus finally reached Vaḷḷikkāvu. There was a certain distance to be walked in order to reach the āśram, including a crossing of the river by dinghy. I walked briskly and raced ahead of my aunt, getting into a boat that left immediately, leaving her to catch the one that was to follow. Thoroughly worried about losing contact with me, she started crying out, "*Makkaḷē*," "*Makkaḷē*" (an affectionate way of calling out 'son').

Reaching the āśram, I blindly dashed to Amma. She was seated in front of the kaḷari at that time. With agony driving me to madness, I fell headlong at Her feet, cupped them with both my hands and started sobbing violently and uncontrollably.

Tvamēva śaraṇam Śivē

O Goddess, You alone are my refuge!

Amma tried to pacify me, caressing my back and trying to lift me up, but I continued to sob, almost wailing loudly, holding on tightly to Her feet. The commotion caused a small flutter, the gathering of devotees and Amma's family members rushing to the scene to find out what had happened, as I learned later.

I do not know how long I continued, but finally Amma comforted me to some semblance of silence. When my sniffling had subsided, She asked, "What happened to you, darling son? Why are you crying? Where has your courage vanished to?"

Hearing Amma's voice and words, I started crying yet again. She could console me only with great difficulty. After a long time, I felt renewed by a sense of peace and inner stability. Amma made me sit by Her side, and then started speaking to me on spiritual life.

I felt as if I had been reborn. With Amma's blessings, I soon became a permanent āśram resident. At that time, there were only three brahmacāris staying in the āśram. They were Br. Uṇṇikṛṣṇan (now Swāmi Turīyāmṛtānanda Puri), Br. Bālagōpāl (now Swāmi Amṛtaswarūpānanda Puri) and Br. Nīlu (now Swāmi Paramātmānanda Puri). I was the fourth brahmacāri to join the āśram and perform spiritual practices under Amma's direct guidance. So, just a few months after I first saw Amma, I was blessed to stay in Her āśram permanently. Thus began a golden chapter in my life.

Kind and loving, yet firm and task-masterly in Her instructions and supervision, Amma would very often remind me of an uncompromising mother determined to raise Her toddling son to spiritual heights. If I have understood and imbibed even an iota of spiritual wisdom, the credit goes to Amma, Her exclusive advice, close supervision and enduring grace, especially all that I received from Her in the early stages.

During those early years, I would spend most of my time in intense *sādhanā* (spiritual practice). Seeing my enthusiasm, every day, Amma would spend a few hours talking to me, answering all the questions I would ask Her, and giving me much advice. I can say without any hesitation whatsoever that the first-hand advice I received from Amma then has shaped my spiritual outlook today.

In the following chapter, I have included just a little of the ambrosial advice that Amma dispensed that day and in the next few days after I arrived at Her āśram and fell at Her feet. These pearls of advice pertain to the principles that enrich and enhance the quality of life.

27

Ambrosial Advice

When I had finally calmed down, Amma gently lifted me up from Her lap and spoke solemn words of wisdom. Noting the change in my outward appearance—my shaven head and ash-smeared forehead and body—Amma said, "Mōnē, *puramalla moṭṭa aṭikkēṇṭatu akamāṇu, manassineyāṇu muṇḍanam ceyyēṇṭatu*"—"Son, it is not the exterior but the interior that has to be tonsured; it is the mind that ought to be clean-shaven." Ācārya Śankara's mordant observation in *Bhaja-gōvindam*—"*Jaṭilō muṇḍī luñchitakēśaḥ / kāṣāyāmbara bahukṛtavēṣaḥ*" (14) ("The aged monk with shaven crown or trimmed hair and strangely attired in saffron robes")—bore immediate comparison, revealing the practical insight of the two Masters. The external shaving is symbolic of the removing of desires; hence their injunction against mere outward show.

Amma added, "Son, outward show has no place in and is extraneous to the path you have chosen. Sādhaks who show off their purpose cannot be considered sincere in their efforts. The seeker of Truth doesn't have anything to gain or lose, since there is nothing that matters beyond the realization of the Self, and once that goal is reached, there is nothing left anymore to look back to or yearn for further. Since the endeavor is one's own and is principally directed for personal spiritual elevation, the need for superfluous expression by way of external display does not arise. Wearing crinkled clothes and smearing holy ash all over the body is mere outward show.

"Being emotionally weak and prone to tears is not befitting of an aspirant. In fact, the spiritual path is meant for the fearless. You ought to dress and act according to the times. Looking at you, others should become inspired to walk the spiritual path.

"People may find fault and criticize an aspirant but you should not take notice of it. If you await a certificate of merit from the world, you will lose the recognition of the Divine. If you have to fight, let it be with your own *vāsanās* (latent tendecies). When a sādhak finds faults externally, he should understand that what he is seeing is only a reflection of his own defects. He should thus strive to remove those shortcomings. If you have to find fault with anyone, let it be with yourself. By criticizing others, the world will not change; we won't change either. In the world, criticism is directed outwards, but in spirituality, criticism is and should be towards oneself only. Then, we can change for the better.

Whereas worldly association relegates one to mortality, love of the divine elevates one to immortality.

"It is folly to fritter away one's life without realizing its aim. Just as every trade has its tools, the body is the means for the business of realizing the Self. One should use it profitably to seek and find the soul, for the very aim of life is the realization of the soul—everlasting Bliss. The endeavor should begin early in life when the body is healthy.

"No one brings anything along with him into this world nor does he take away anything from here. The only thing that we actually bring and take away is '*karmaphalam*,' the fruits of action. Any human being who is free from the bondage of karma is immortal, immortality being our birthright.

"Material gain and loss are inevitable. If this is understood, you will not wilt in sorrow. Peace of mind is the real wealth. One should be able to observe thoughts as they pass through the mind, only seeing them, and not identifying with any of them.

"There is a thrill in witnessing the flow of a swift river; similar is the joy one can derive from being a witness to the happenings in life. You should train the mind to remain a witness to thoughts. It will strengthen the mind. Those who are enlightened do not perceive evil anywhere. Seeing the faults of others is not a strength, but a weakness. If one is constantly focused on the weaknesses of others, when will he find time to reflect on his own?

"Don't we see the impartial receiving appreciation in everyday life? Even in the courts of law, we find importance given to witnesses. Only as observers can the world be enjoyed. A teacher asked a student a question. The student, who knew the answer, was nervous and started mumbling. The rest of the class, who were onlookers, started giggling, making fun of the boy. Had any one of them been in his shoes, the situation would have been no different. Therefore, we need to cultivate *sākṣi bhāva* (witness attitude), thereby avoiding over-indulgence, in all our activities.

"There were many thefts in a residential colony. The residents appointed a watchman to catch the thieves. This halted the spate of stealing incidents, proving that the mere presence of a watchman acts as a deterrent to burglars. Similarly, if the intellect sharpened by discrimination is used to observe the thoughts, it will eventually lead to a strengthening of the mind."

I was amazed thinking of how a person with only a few years of formal education could comment on a profound topic like this in such simple and lucid terms. In contrast, mediocre scholars explaining much simpler subjects tend to make them more complex, their explanations and elaborations revealing their keenness to parade their intellectual skills rather than a sincere interest to help others understand the subject. In contrast, when Masters impart the multi-faceted aspects of life to others, it is done with the earnestness to convey the truth, to make sure that others understand them, and do not in any way try to project their own eminence. Their words of wisdom abound in compassion and mirror true selflessness. Being aware of their true Self, they remain steeped in eternal bliss. However, they are also deeply concerned about those who are sunk in ignorance and are thus wasting their lives. This concern manifests as a steady flow of compassion and mercy, and a deep yearning to make others like themselves.

Some so-called pundits ask if Amma has studied the scriptures. Such a question is akin to asking a squirrel scurrying up and down the tree without missing a step, from which university it earned its tree-climbing degree. This doubt, voiced by those stuck firmly to the ground and incapable of taking even one step up the tree, reveals the ignorance of the questioner. It is said that the Vēdas are God's exhalation. Wondering if Amma, the very incarnation of divinity, has studied the scriptures is sheer folly.

The Self can never be an object of issue or concern for anyone. Problems and complexities arise only because of issues of 'belonging' to oneself. The notion that the physical body belongs to 'me' is the key to all misunderstanding. In actual fact, 'I' (Self) transcends the body, mind and intellect. Confusion vanishes the moment the sense of mine-ness is removed. 'I' minus 'mine-ness' = Almighty; Man minus vāsanās = Vāsudēva (Lord Viṣṇu, the all-pervasive).

Those who only speak on consciousness make it complex, but those who are one with it keep it simple. The swimming coach who trains others enjoys the session and finds fulfillment in teaching his students how to swim. In contrast, someone trying to teach swimming verbally finds the task complicated, and the trainees find the instructions tortuous and long-winded, resulting in their never learning how to swim.

Simplicity is the very nature of the wise, for whom it is inherent and never forced. Unlike contrived actions, the magnetic charm of simplicity attracts everyone. When plainness is innate in the conduct, how can there arise a need to demonstrate it? It effortlessly becomes a part and parcel of the actions. To a mother, carrying a child on her side is easy, whereas for others, it is an effort.

The Self in itself is simple, but when associated with senses seems complex for the ignorant. When the Self is recognized for its essential purity, i.e. when the seeming link between the body, mind and intellect, and the Self is recognized as illusory, complexities wane and the whole matter becomes simple. Impurity is the impediment; purity is the way out.

Amma once said, "Children, isn't the term 'practical Vēdānta' self-explanatory, and doesn't it indicate a topic that should be *practiced* instead of debated or preached? The time taken to practice it is not meant to be wasted on lecturing about it. Those who utilize the energy in deed instead of word are the ones who practice Vēdānta. Through their actions, they impart the knowledge of Vēdānta to people at large."

Amma elucidated the point through a parable about a small family consisting of a father, mother and daughter. The father, who was very kind and simple, was liked by all in the village because of his willingness to help the poor and needy. However, he was neither a regular visitor to the temple nor well-versed in the sacred chants and hymns.

The mother, on the other hand, was religious, a regular visitor to the temple, singing and chanting hymns, and reading scriptural texts, but she never believed in following the code of conduct inside the temple. She would cut the queue of devotees to place herself in front for viewing the deity during the ārati, and would harshly berate devotees who obstructed her view of the deity.

While the father would keep calm in the face of adversities in day-to-day life, the mother would cry and grumble before the deity, complaining that despite her sincere worship she had to face adversities. Other devotees were often confused by the waywardness in her devotion. The daughter who believed that the mother was a true devotee did not understand why she had to go through these trying times.

It was then that God appeared to the daughter in a dream and explained the reason: "In your house, the true devotee is your father. Love and concern for fellow-beings are, in a nutshell, the true measure of devotion. Listening to the sorrows and sufferings of others, pacifying them and extending help are the hallmarks of a true devotee."

Concluding the story, Amma said, "Vēdānta is what can be made practicable in everyday life. Amma wonders why the distinction between the physical and the spiritual arose. In earlier times, spirituality was an inherent part of life. Grandmother tales, norms of social conduct, the school curriculum and moral values, which were woven into the fabric of life, helped to sustain it; it was not something people strived for deliberately. In due course of time, the minds of people became less and less subtle, and the relevance of spirituality diminished. That is how it became estranged from daily life. Now, if someone chants a mantra before eating, meditates or does some japa, people are likely to say that he is religious or spiritual. But this was the norm a long time ago. To live a life following the higher values dictated by one's faith is spirituality."

A question that devotees often ask Amma is, "What is the relevance of spirituality?"

Amma's reply runs thus: "Children, the urge to ask this question is good. If there was any one object in this world that could ensure complete satisfaction, everyone would rely on it. But there is no such object. We can see that no one can attain absolute satisfaction from any other source than God. Spirituality is single-pointedness; the lack of it is worldliness.

"The choice of making life joyful or otherwise is in our hands. The path of Truth not only gives happiness to the individual; through him, society at large is also benefited. A seeker may have to sacrifice everything, but with Self-realization, he attains completeness and fulfillment.

"The failure to achieve one's desired goals brings unhappiness and dissatisfaction, whereas Self-realization ushers in contentment and bliss. Is there anything in the world that we will not lose after we achieve it? This is true even of the body. But for those who have realized themselves, there is nothing left to lose.

"Man thinks that he is the crown of creation. But his real superiority lies in the God-given power of discrimination. If he uses this gift to take him to the Supreme, then only is he worthy of being called the crown of creation. Otherwise, in many respects, other beings are superior to him. If we observe nature, we will be amazed by the astonishing variety of its beauty as well as the diversity of its strengths and skills. A predatory bird that can pinpoint minute movements from miles above; a snake that can sense sounds vibrations; the startling beauty of colors and patterns that mark the fauna at large; or a dog gifted with the keen sense of smell and the ability to anticipate natural disasters—these are just some of the traits that human beings lack. If man does not use discriminative intelligence, which is exclusive to him, for seeking the Truth, how is he superior to animals?

"Selflessness can be seen in all of nature's creations. Each and every cell of the body is relentlessly engaged in unselfish service. From the time of birth, every part of the body behaves selflessly, and this behavior continues unremittingly until death without any expectation of return. In effect, they symbolize sacrifice and renunciation. Trees, creepers and plants exist principally to cater to birds and animals. Leaves give way to flowers, which in turn are replaced by fruits, which ripen to provide food to the hungry. Isn't renunciation the fundamental principle underlying these processes? A monk is one who gives away love in alms. He should be broad-minded and impartial. As far as he is concerned, the world belongs to him and he belongs to the world. When dedicated at the altar of humanitarianism, monkhood leads to Godhood."

In the earlier days, I often used to see Amma looking at the sky and seldom at the earth; the reason, I surmised, was the unity perceivable in the skies in comparison with the diversity that marked the earth. We can often see conflicts stemming from ego-based issues in husband-wife partnerships but rarely can we find it in mother-children relations; this is because a mother's conviction that the children are her own, that they are an innate part of her (in principle, herself), is rooted in pure egolessness. That is why an evolved soul, who regards the whole of creation as an extension of himself, is never in conflict with anyone.

Touching on Love, Amma said, "All of nature symbolizes love. The wind flows, lovingly caressing the good and the evil alike, regardless of class, creed and color. A river flows for and serves all humanity—both saint and criminal bathe in it; a leper and a healthy person use it; many pollute the river; many cleanse themselves by bathing in it. Whether used reverentially or otherwise, the river is not concerned. Thus the various objects of nature are emblematic of sacrifice, love and selflessness. With its incessant activity for the good of humanity, nature is a shining example for us to emulate.

"Why is that although we bow down to the Sun and Moon gods, we have not acquired the impartiality, egolessness and witness attitude of these benign planets? The selfless are worthy of grace; the selfish heart is an obstruction to its flow. Altruistic conduct is spirituality. There is none who can be considered totally good or totally bad. We should learn to see only the goodness of others. Children, the Self in everyone is divine. Having compassion towards all is divine love.

"Once we attain Godhood, we will see everything that comes our way as His will. Because of our craving for relatively trivial matters of life, we overlook the need to rely on the divine. One should cry and yearn for the grace of God. Tears in worldly life are caused by sorrow and grief, whereas tears in spiritual life are caused by the yearning for God."

On one occasion, while speaking about contemporary issues that moved Amma to compassion, I asked Her, "Amma, do these matters really bother You?"

Amma replied, "However high and forcefully the tsunami waves flow over a tender coconut, it can touch only the exterior; the water inside the coconut remains untouched and as pure and sweet as ever. Amma is like the water in a tender coconut. She has no sorrow of Her own, but the sorrows of others become Her sorrows. No other factor except our own mind is capable of arresting or preventing our happiness. Joys and sorrows are the creation of the mind; in the absence of both, what remains is bliss. When many tried to accuse and tarnish me, Amma never felt bad about it because I knew I was Bliss itself, and thus it did not make me sad.

"When actions are not dedicated to a higher cause, they lead one to think, 'I am doing everything. All these are the results of my actions.' Instead, if we think, 'Everything is due to Divine Grace' or 'All happens according to God's will,' then the ego vanishes, and a spirit of total surrender takes over, the 'me' (Jīva) replaced by the 'Me' (Paramātma).

"All material gains stand in the way of spiritual progress; they veil the path. Actions can bring material gains, which tend to increase our attachment to them and inflate our ego. Son, try to learn from experience because each one of them is a treasure. No one has succeeded in resolving sorrow through physical gains; those who have pursued the spiritual path have never come to regret it.

"For those who perceive only diversity in the world, devotion and knowledge are separate. But the enlightened, who see the unity in diversity, know that devotion and knowledge are one and the same; they are complementary to each other. Devotion is obedience to the Guru, to whom the disciple should behave with candor and solemnity; conduct that is conducive to taking one to the Supreme Goal is also devotion.

"Without the grace of the Guru, it is not possible to overcome one's vāsanās. Although they are the creation of the

Jīva, it is the Guru who knows the subtle nature of vāsanās, not the disciple. Whereas an immature disciple deems a Guru's punishment as a curse, a true disciple considers it a blessing in disguise. The outcome of His treatment depends on how the disciple receives it. Divinity is realized and liberation is attained only through the Guru's grace. The Guru, who is free of all desire, is verily the abode of Liberation."

na gurōradhikam tattvam na gurōradhikam tapaḥ
tattvajñānāt param nāsti tasmai śrī guravē namaḥ
There is no principle greater than the Guru, no austerity greater than the Guru, and there is nothing greater than knowledge of the supreme principle. Salutations to that Guru who is of the form of the supreme principle.

(Guru Gītā, 74)

Part Four

Acceptance

28

Selfless Service

Bhāratam has traditionally laid great emphasis on *sēva* (selfless service). Historically, sēva had a religious dimension, and it influenced many aspects of human life. Guru Nānak underscored the significance of sēva, saying that whether "recluse, hero, celibate or sanyāsi, none will earn merit without devoted service." Khalil Gibran averred, "You give little when you give of your possessions. It is when you give of yourself that you truly give." Śrī Rāmakṛṣṇa Paramahamsa stressed the importance of service as the very basis of spiritual life, and held that the unity of existence stemmed principally from this understanding. Once, when he went to meet Īśwaracandra Vidyāsāgar, the renowned reformer, Śrī Rāmakṛṣṇa is said to have greeted Vidyāsāgar as a '*siddhapuruṣa*.'

Hearing such high praise from the Master, Vidyāsāgar asked, "How can I be a *siddha* (Self-realized person) without sādhanā?"

Pointing towards the assorted gathering, which included students, a child widow and a social outcast among others,

waiting for help, the Master said, "You selflessly serve others whereas the so-called holy men strive for their own liberation. If this doesn't make you a siddha, what does?"

Service is spiritual practice, a noble venture, that can take us to the goal of Self-realization. As far as a seeker of Truth is concerned, every action, no matter what, ought to take one closer to the ultimate goal.

Selflessness is only for those who realize the Self. There is no selflessness without the Self.

Amma says, "*Advaitam* (non-duality) is the basic truth that should find expression in our lives. When the left hand is injured, the right one caresses and comforts it because both are parts of the same body and hence one. In the same way, to love and serve others as your Self is, in a nutshell, pragmatic Advaitam."

The first thing Amma did after I joined the āśram was to hand me a broomstick. There was nothing more to say. For the next 10 years, I served as the sweeper of the āśram. I was aware that in handing me the broomstick, Amma wanted me to clean not just the āśram grounds; more importantly, it was symbolic of the need to cleanse my own, inner environment. That is the spiritual purpose of sēva or karma: to remove one's impurities.

Apart from sweeping, one of my other sēvas was in the cowshed, where I worked with Damayanti-amma. I remember how, after bathing the cows daily, I would take great delight in smearing the cows' forehead with sacred ash and anointing them with vermilion. Br. Rao (now Swāmi Amṛtātmānanda Puri) also used to do sēva in the cowshed, cleaning it as well as bathing and feeding the cows. Before joining the āśram, he was a successful businessman. Watching him discharge his duties in the cowshed, I would reflect on the transformation that Amma brought about in the lives of so many people. All the sanyāsis and sanyāsinis had humble beginnings at the āśram. In fact, those who join the āśram are, in general, initially assigned sēvas that are menial, by worldly standards. However, in spirituality, no task is superior or inferior to another. Any action performed selflessly confers mental purity, through which one attains the Truth.

I have heard the story of a young man, who, drawn to the spiritual life, decided to become a novitiate. In his new life, he had several duties to perform. Apart from these, the Guru would, once in a while, summon him and direct him to sweep the meditation hall and surrounding premises. Sensing his reluctance to do menial jobs, the Guru said, "You dislike it because you are not used to sweeping and cleaning. You think you deserve to do only white-collar jobs?" Often, the revolting mind will acquiesce externally; he will execute the job to capture the Guru's attention in the fond hope of being appreciated for his hard work.

Hailing from an affluent family, the novitiate found cleaning with a broom an embarrassing task. Since the Guru wanted the āśram to be spick-and-span, the job had to be done with immense care. However, the pride in his elite upbringing often dominated his thoughts. What if someone he knew came up while he was sweeping? But he had to contend with the hard taskmaster that his Guru was.

Caught between the devil and the deep blue sea, the disciple tried to find a means to satisfy the Guru and avoid being seen by others while sweeping. He would endeavor to finish the cleaning early in the morning before devotees arrived to attend the services. Since the Guru would give him other jobs at random, he was not always successful in avoiding people who knew him. As a result, he would avoid cleaning around the gate.

This ruse did not work very often since the schedules varied, and the disciple would be caught by a relative right in the middle of sweeping. His mind working overtime to safeguard his pride would come to his help; he would tell his relative, "The people who are supposed to do the cleaning are away, and after all, cleanliness is very important, and since the Guru insists on cleanliness, I thought I would do it myself."

Once, caught yet again in sweeping, he swore under his breath, "Why does this guy have to come right at this time!"

Very often, when an acquaintance appeared while he cleaned, the disciple would pretend that he had not seen him or her, but the situation would worsen when the visitor would tap his back to get his attention and say, "Why are *you* sweeping? Isn't there anyone else to do this job? Where is the Guru? Is he not around?"

The disciple, his pride now badly wounded, would respond, "Oh, the Guru is around. That's why I have to put up with this!"

A group of elderly females who knew him then came to the āśram while he was sweeping. Seeing him with a broom, they reacted sympathetically. "Oh dear, are you meant to do this? Seeing you like this makes us feel very sad. Had we been healthy, we could have done it ourselves."

Overhearing these remarks, the Master summoned the disciple and said, "Having chosen the spiritual path, you should seek the compassion only of the Divine and not the comfort offered by the external world. You ought to be an example for all outside and that is also why I am training you like this."

But with time, his own sensitivity to unclean surroundings would make the disciple uneasy, the hidden voice of the Guru pointing it out. He also noticed that whenever he procrastinated, the cleaning would soon be carried out by someone else, the will of the Master finding expression naturally.

Amma continued, "We should perform our duties as much as possible without attracting the attention of the Guru. We should not try to involve the Guru or others in our efforts, or try to impress them with our work. If one desires to seek the love and grace of the Guru or God, he should dispassionately work with the conviction that the Guru can discern each of his thought, action and intention. Such a person is mature and worthy of carrying out the tasks of the Guru, and God will be pleased with him. One should obey the advice of the Guru. The Guru lives only for the disciples.

"Among the ways to gain divine grace, the greatest is adopting the attitude of a servant. The heart of the devotee is essentially an offering at the feet of the Lord. An offering, once made, after all, cannot be taken back. Like a spider continuing to weave the web even while falling down, a devotee should steadfastly hold on to the Lord's feet even through adversities. Children, real service to Amma is doing your duties selflessly with satisfaction and joy.

"More than revering Amma, you should also strive to become Amma yourself. You should become the symbol of Truth, the very embodiment of eternal bliss!"

29

Sweet Spats

I still fondly recall the early days in the āśram. The few disciples who were staying with Amma then used to go to Her for the smallest things, and in the child's liberty with the Mother, would quarrel with Her sometimes. There was stiff competition among us, but this was in making spiritual progress. I was especially over-zealous in this matter, impatient to attain Self-realization. In my arduous sādhanā, whenever I encountered impediments, I would get immensely irritated and upset. This would inadvertently push me to take it out on Amma.

Picking up my knapsack and taking off with no destination in mind was my novel form of protest. However, a little more than a mile away, at the Vaḷḷikkāvu junction, the aroma of hot, freshly prepared *'vaṭa'* (a South Indian fried savory) and steam-baked ground nuts from the eateries there would arrest my progress, a sudden brainwave inspiring me to take some of it to Amma, and thus reconcile with Her. Returning barely an hour or two later, I would give Her the snacks, the reunion evoking laughter all around. She would affectionately say, "I knew how far you would go!" Amma would often laughingly recount this incident to devotees, highlighting my tendency to sulk and the way I would pick up my rucksack and leave in disapproval.

In a similar instance that followed, I took a trifle more time than usual to return, and when I did, I found Amma looking distressed. That is when I realized the gravity of my impetuous conduct. She said poignantly, "Where can you go?" In a choked voice, She asked, "Would the combined love of millions of mothers equal mine?"

Once, in a moment of inspiration, I started sharing what I had read about how a disciple should conduct himself before the Guru with Br. Rāmakṛṣṇa (now Swāmi Rāmakṛṣṇānanda Puri), who listened very attentively to what I was saying. Barely five minutes after I left him, I went to see Amma. Within moments, I started quarreling noisily with Her over some issue. Hearing the loud sounds of an altercation, Br. Rāmakṛṣṇa came to investigate, and saw me quarrelling with Amma! So much for my high philosophy! It is difficult to practice what one preaches.

On yet another occasion, following a difference of opinion with Amma, I got tetchy and left the āśram in a huff. It took me the whole day to feel the pangs of separation from *Jagat Janani*, the Universal Mother, and think of returning from my escapade. When I came back in the twilit hours,

I found an anguished Amma waiting for me. Sobbing, She reached out, clasped me in Her arms, and held me for some time. In a voice filled with emotion, She said, "Son! Can you ever separate yourself and be away from me? Has there ever been a life in the past when you have not been with me? However many more lives may follow, Vēṇu will belong to me!" I was deeply touched by Amma's revealing words.

30

Primordial Pose

During my early days in the Amṛtapuri āśram, Amma blessed me with a profound experience that revealed Her cosmic eminence. The setting was a tiny hut and, the center of focus, an exceedingly beautiful idol of Lord Kṛṣṇa, rendered all the more attractive by adornments. Being an ardent devotee of Kṛṣṇa, I used to take great pains to beautify the idol during my worship and, as was my wont, would spend time gazing at it without blinking, enjoying the exceptional beauty of the decorated image. I would delve into the subtler attributes of the Lord, and thus my worship would gradually induce in me a state of absorption.

It was on one of these occasions, when I was lost in adoration of my Lord, that Amma walked in behind me. She stood at the door, leaning a little inside and looking at me. Seeing the ardor of my devotion, She smiled. Noticing Amma, I sprang up from my seat and prostrated at Her feet. Pointing to my Kṛṣṇa idol, I asked Her a silly question. "Amma! Do you see my Kṛṣṇa standing?"

Amma spontaneously shot back: "Wasn't it after I stood up that your Kṛṣṇa stood up?" Her utterance startled me. When I had recovered sufficiently to take in that mystic utterance, I reckoned that what She meant was that She was already in existence before the Divine incarnated in the form of Lord Kṛṣṇa.

According to the Upaniṣadic perspective, in the beginning, there was only the Absolute, 'the One without a second,' or pure consciousness. This universe of names and forms originated from that Supreme Being. When Amma uses the first person pronoun 'I,' She is speaking from the state of universal consciousness (*Paramātma bhāva*).

Amma's spontaneous utterance echoes well-known scriptural statements, some of which are given below:

> *avajānanti mām mūḍhā mānuṣīm tanumāśritam*
> *param bhāvamajānanto mama bhūtamahēśvaram*
>
> Not knowing My transcendental nature, fools misunderstand Me, the Supreme Lord of all beings, as having assumed a human body.
>
> *(Bhagavad Gītā, 9.11)*
>
> *Janmādyasya yataḥ*
>
> That from which the creation, preservation and dissolution of the entire universe take place is Brahman, the Supreme Being.
>
> *(Brahmasūtram, 2)*

Sadēva sōmyēdamagra āsīdēkamēvādvitīyam
Before creation, O amiable one, there was only pure, non-dual existence, One without a second or parts.
(Chāndōgyōpaniṣad, 6.2.1)

As if struck by lightning, Amma's words slowly converged in my mind, revealing the profundity of Her statement. While I tried to recover from the bewildering jolt, Amma chuckled meaningfully, and left the hut.

I was awe-struck by the intense depth of Amma's statement, revealing Her true stature as Supreme Consciousness Itself. 'Amma' is not merely a word—it is an experience.

Ādi Śankarācārya in *Saundarya Laharī* is rapturous in his veneration of the Universal Mother:

Mahāmāyā viśvam bhramayati parabrahmamahiṣī
Mahāmāyā (the illusory power), the divine consort of Parabrahma, perplexes the entire universe. (97)

Every moment that we remain taken in by body consciousness, forgetting that we are all truly divine, we are deceiving ourselves.

Once, a devotee asked me, "Swāmiji, where is Amma now?" it being usual for people to inquire about Amma's whereabouts in view of Her frequent touring.

I replied, "Amma is there now, where She is all the time!"

31

Extraordinary Exegete

On a later occasion, I asked Amma about the states of ecstatic bliss She was often in, Her inner beatitude. She said, "The soulful experience comes from an intense and continuous contemplation of the Divine. The seeker of Truth eventually realizes the soul's eternal unity with all perceived objects. He identifies with that unbroken existence, and merges with it. No amount of verbal description can explain the phenomenon except that the sense of duality gives way to an awareness of non-duality, evoking a rapturous joy beyond words. This experience manifests itself in a variety of exalted moods."

Explanations can never purport to be the Truth, which transcends reasoning and justification. Volumes may be written on maternal love, but they can never compare with the experience of people who have understood it through experience.

The phrase "*Viśvam darpaṇadṛśyamāna nagarītulyam nijāntargatam*" in *Śrī Dakṣiṇāmūrti Stōtram* describes the basic nature of a liberated soul like Amma, who beholds the universe in the mind in the same way as one beholds in a mirror the innumerable images of an urban sprawl.

In an interview on the eve of Her 58th birthday, in response to a thought-provoking query from a journalist, "What makes You happy?" Amma used a down-to-earth analogy to explain Her true nature: "Amma's happiness is not one that comes one moment and leaves the next! Can anyone ever say that he will breathe only in the company of his friends and not in the presence of his enemies? Breathing is a continuing, natural process, and so is Amma's happiness—always the same under all circumstances. In effect, the sorrows of others are mine, and their happiness is mine, too. They reflect in me as if in a mirror, although there is a state beyond this level of experience, a realm that transcends both happiness and sorrow. We can bring ourselves to love and serve simultaneously only if we attempt to rise above joy and grief. Only when the mind becomes as expansive as the sky is it possible to comprehend the unity of existence."

Once, while talking to a few devotees, a woman who was undergoing the trauma of divorce started wailing uncontrollably. She said, "Swāmiji, I can't take it anymore. I'm unable to respond to anything in any other way except by crying for everything."

I said, "Crying is a becoming way of responding. However, when you do that to a selfish and weak person, he is likely to take advantage of it, but when you cry before a selfless person like Amma, She will be moved to behave compassionately towards you."

We often lament, "No one understands me!" Everyone wants to be understood. Therefore, we should realize that others also expect to be understood by us. Are we trying to do that? To carry the burden of the heart by oneself is obstinacy whereas to surrender it to the divine is wisdom.

Spiritual flowering follows the weeding out of impurities, just as the dispelling of darkness leaves the seeker's mind radiant. When a room filled with superfluous objects is cleared out, the recovered space ushers in a sense of spaciousness and brightness, leading one to feel that light has entered the room. By the same logic, when the mind is rid of darkness in the form of impurities, the mind becomes radiant, "like a thousand suns," as rhetorically expressed in the scriptures.

When the sun of unified consciousness dawns, the darkness of duality flees, and the waves of 'I' and 'mine' ebb away, leading to the awareness that none of the material objects we claim to own—such as home, family and children, and belongings—are ours in reality. That which we construe as having lost is not 'ours.' The true 'I' or 'me' has nothing to lose. Is it not the sense of duality then that triggers the feeling of loss? What we should strive to lose instead is the conditioning that has led us to think we are individuated entities. To quote Henry David Thoreau, "It is only when we forget all our learning that we begin to know."

Like the proverbial sage who, on being threatened with beheading by an invading emperor, calmly rejoined, "I will then witness my own beheading," or the monk, who on being caught by an attacking lion, continued chanting, "*SōSham, sōSham*" ("I am He / God"), the Self-realized one knows that even after death, 'I' does not change, only what belongs to 'my' body.

A gripping event in the life of Śrī Śankara provides a fine illustration here. The chief of the Kāpālikās (a sect of wandering ascetics who worship Lord Śiva in the form of Kapāli, the bearer of the skull-bowl) had obtained from the Lord a boon: to attain the Lord's abode in his human frame. He was told that the wish would be fulfilled if he could perform a sacrifice of offering the head of a king or an all-knowing person at the altar of Kapāli. The Kāpālikā approached Śankara, narrated to him his ambition, and said, "You are a man of renunciation, without attachment to the body; you live only for the good of others. Sages like Dadhīci[37] gladly gave others their impermanent physical

37 A sage who won eternal glory by allowing Indra (chief of the celestials) to take his backbone out and shape it into a deadly weapon to win a war against the demons.

body. Be gracious to give me your head so that I can fulfill my vow by offering it to Kapāli."

Śrī Śankara, who was full of mercy, said, "Gladly shall I give you my head. What greater glory can there be than offering this body, which is transient, for the benefit of another?" Granting the wish of the Kāpālikā, the *Ācārya* (Preceptor), however, cautioned him, "But you should take my head away in absolute secrecy when my disciples are away." He added, "I shall come at the appointed time for the execution."

At the predetermined hour, the Kāpālikā led Śrī Śankara to a secluded spot replete with eerie and grotesque trappings. Armed members of the clan were in attendance for the formal sacrifice. The great non-dualist sat down to meditate and soon became immersed in Supreme Bliss. Just as the Kāpālikā was about to bring the sword down on the Ācārya's head, Padmapāda, the illustrious disciple of the monk, appeared on the scene. Having acquired supernatural powers through his worship of Lord Narasimha,[38] he had divined the heinous plot of the tribal chief. Invoking the terrifying form of Narasimha and transforming himself into it, Padmapāda roared, charged at the Kāpālikā, and slew both him and the armed clansmen. Hearing the commotion, the

38 The half-man, half-lion form, the fourth incarnation of Lord Viṣṇu.

other disciples rushed to the place to find the Ācārya in samādhi and the corpse of Kāpālikā lying nearby. When Śankara emerged from his samādhi, he found Padmapāda in the fearsome form of Narasimha. The Ācārya then sang hymns to pacify the Lord.

This extraordinary exegete, who practiced what he preached, had offered himself to be beheaded, demonstrating his spirit of self-sacrifice and boundless compassion, and upholding the universal truth of unified existence, extolled in *Nirvāṇaṣaṭkam*:

> *manōbuddhyahankāracittāni nāham*
> *na ca śrōtrajihvē na ca ghrāṇanētrē*
> *na ca vyōmabhūmirna tējō na vāyu-*
> *ścidānandarūpaḥ śivōSham, śivōSham*
>
> I am neither the mind, the intellect, the ego, nor the memory. Nor am I the ears, the tongue, the nose or the eyes. I am not ether, air, fire, water or earth. I am of the nature of pure consciousness and bliss. I am Śiva! I am Śiva!

This evergreen hymn, composed by the venerable Śrī Śankara, reminds me of an incident that took place during my early days in the āśram. One morning, I was reciting it musically and loudly as is my wont. The words '*śivōSham, śivōSham*' ('I am Śiva, pure consciousness') were resounding in my heart, since the term used to give me a lot of inner joy. That morning, while I was intoning the hymn, Amma walked in and arrested my musical rendering of the prayer with this observation: "Son, if you keep repeating '*śivōSham, śivōSham,*' you will not attain anything! If an egg is to hatch, the mother hen has to incubate it. Like chicks, which break out from their shells only after a long, patient wait under their mother's wings, the seeker can evolve only through rigorous sādhanā under the guidance of a preceptor. He cannot evolve merely by proclaiming '*śivōSham, śivōSham,*' just as a chick cannot become a hen by mere declaration. Pure, innocent and whole-hearted love for the Lord, which culminates in total surrender, is the best and simplest approach. It is better to chant '*DāsōSham, dāsōSham*' ('I am Your servant') in the initial stages of one's spiritual sādhanā."

To drive home the point, Amma said, "Can a person being subjected to physical assault bear it if he keeps chanting 'śivōSham?' If he can withstand the bodily torture, then it is fine. Otherwise, what is the purpose of repeating 'śivōSham?'"

Amma's vision surpasses all known limits. Her wisdom is infinitely rich, like that of a *ṛṣi*.[39] A Ṛg-Vēdic mantra states the case thus: "*darśam nu viśvadarśatam*"—"I have seen the Creator." (1.25.18)

39 Seers to whom mantras were revealed in deep meditation.

32

Coherent Compassion

Once, I called on Amma in Her room when She was informally talking to a group of devotees on the necessity of being sensitive to all living beings. She delved at length on the importance of having an attitude informed by empathy and a sense of humanitarianism. "Love and compassion can never be stressed enough to seekers on the spiritual path. When we see the sufferings of others, our heart should not remain hard like a rock, but should melt like butter. Realizing the immanence of God in everything is the end; striving to see Him in everything is the means," Amma said.

After everyone else had left Her room, She told me about an incident that took place some time before in the āśram. Once, at around midnight, Amma heard the continual lowing of a calf from the cowshed in the distance. The intermittent cries of the calf were full of distress, and they pierced Her heart. She instantly divined the cause: the cow that had given birth to the calf had died.

Amma obtained a baby-feeding bottle, filled it with milk, fastened a nipple, and brought some extra milk in case it was needed. Accompanied by one or two people, Amma took a torchlight and hurried down to the cowshed. Her guess proved correct: the mother cow was dead, and the newborn was ravenous. Amma sat close to the calf and, caressing it very lovingly, fed it milk from the bottle, taking the calf into Her lap and whispering sweet nothings to make it feel loved.

Amma spent a long time coaxing and cajoling the calf with intimate maternal monologues, and then made arrangements for its well-being before returning to Her room. "A mother's arms are made of tenderness, and children sleep soundly in them" said Victor Hugo.

Amma's compassion extends to all living beings, as I learned from personal experience, shortly after joining the āśram. Once, giving me a vessel of *pāyasam* (sweet pudding), Damayanti-amma smilingly told me to offer it at the Yogīśwaran altar;[40] I smiled when I saw the twinkle in her eye. We both knew that I loved pāyasam, and that I would eat it after having placed it at the altar for a token 30 minutes. In those days, when food was not always forthcoming, pāyasam was a rare treat and savored all the more for it. Happily carrying the vessel, I walked to the altar and placed it there. Realizing that I needed to cover the vessel, I looked around

40 The tiny altar, located right in front of the kaḷari, commemorating an ancestor from Amma's family.

and saw a very small tree with a few big leaves. Without a second thought, I plucked a leaf. At that very moment, I heard a voice booming out, "Vēṇu!" Even before I looked up, I knew who it was: Amma. Her resounding voice, now edged with a painful sharpness, had shocked the life out of me! When had She come?

"How could you pluck the leaf?" began Amma. "From the fact that the tree is growing, can't you tell that it is palpitating with life, just as you are? How can you be so cruel as to tear a leaf from this small tree? Don't you realize how much pain it is in? How would you feel if someone tore off one of your limbs?"

Once the initial shock had worn off, I realized that Amma could see the life in the tree as palpably as we see external objects; for Her, it was not an inference, but a perceptible reality. However, knowing that I lacked this inner vision, She had appealed to my sense of reason. I had failed miserably in both.

Amma then walked to the tree. Her face reflected pain and empathy. When She reached the tree, Amma began caressing it gently and, with utmost love in Her voice, started speaking to the tree, apologizing on my behalf for having caused it pain. After some time, She fixed Her gaze on me and, in a deeply hurt voice, said, "Don't ever repeat this mistake again."

This whole episode took place during a darśan day, and was watched by many devotees. Yet, I did not feel any embarrassment. Instead, Amma's words were a real eye-opener for me, and I pledged then and there never to hurt any plant or tree. I have never forgotten the lesson She taught me that day, and have never plucked even one leaf since then. What had begun as a rebuke had given way to a plea. I realized that when mahātmas teach, the teaching issues from their heart to enter the heart of a receptive disciple, effecting a transformation. In contrast, lesser teachers speak from their heads, and their intention to teach is often vitiated by their secret desire to impress.

In those days, I had yet to learn how much more there was to Amma's compassion than meets the eye. Like every other divine quality that sparkles brightly in Her, Amma's compassion is multi-faceted. The following incident highlighted one such aspect for me.

Once, in the early days, an emaciated-looking man appeared in the āśram. From the tattered rags that clung to his gaunt frame, it was clear that he was a beggar. Seeing me, he stretched out his begging bowl and, in a piteous voice, asked for some money. Touched by his abject plight, I immediately went off to get some coins. When I was returning, I saw Amma. Noticing that I had something in my hand, She asked me what I was holding. Pointing to the beggar standing in the distance, I told Her that I was going to give him some money. Amma looked at him for a few moments. Then, turning to me, She said, "Don't give him any money!" Amma's tone and manner were forbidding. I was a little taken aback by Her unyielding stance. Where was Her characteristic compassion? Notwithstanding my misgivings, I knew better than to disobey Her.

That evening, when I went to the seashore for meditation, I saw many villagers gathered around someone. Going near, I realized that it was the beggar; some of the villagers had beaten him up for smoking marijuana. The sight of someone consuming intoxicants in their village had offended the value system of the natives. I then realized why Amma had forbidden me from giving him money. Her all-knowing gaze had understood what the man would have done with the money.

The next day, when this person returned to the āśram, Amma, in Her compassion, directed me to give him some food.

This incident taught me that Amma's compassion can take various guises. In this instance, Her concern had taken the form of 'tough love,' so as to prevent the man from digging himself deeper into the pit of addiction, and committing more unrighteous acts. Amma has said that closing our eyes to *adharma* (unrighteousness) or encouraging it is unrighteous.

Those who perceive all creation as One are the ones who see it in its true perspective. Amma often reassures us, "Children, Amma is always with you." We should ask ourselves, though, if we are always with Her. To be with Amma always is to be dharmic in our words and deeds in every moment.

33

Real Rationalism

Real faith, in my opinion, is accepting the word of the Master without question, even if it be on a subject in which the seeker has no knowledge or experience. He earnestly strives to follow the path, believing that such advice will lead him to spiritual liberation.

Sadly, those who question the words of the Masters, priding themselves on their rationalism, are often the ones praised for their superior intelligence. Such rationalization, analysis or explanation is necessary only for the gross intellect, whereas the faithful accept the Master's words readily and thus tread the subtle path.

There is nothing wrong with doubting or rationalization, provided they are motivated by a sincere search for the Truth. However, the purer the seeker's heart becomes, the subtler his intellect becomes, the lesser his doubts become, the less he relies on rationalization, and the more he begins to apprehend the Truth in the form of experience.

Only one who has a high level of purity and subtlety can accept the Master's words readily without question. Such people are superior in all respects because they reach their objective easily.

In other fields, rationalization is overvalued; not only that, more often than not, the preceptor will not readily share all his knowledge, fearing that the student may surpass him. In contrast, in spirituality, the Master expects his disciples to evolve and become like Him.

As with any constructive and noble system, which invariably attracts a parallel force that tries to invalidate it, spiritual science also has its detractors. The gross intellect, capable only of recognizing and admiring the material aspects of life, always cries foul of spiritual tenets and the happiness they bestow, even challenging their validity. Attempts by the so-called rationalists with selfish interests to misrepresent the spirit of the scriptures and alter the true import of the term 'Vēdānta' have always been in vogue, but these very attempts only serve to highlight its eternal glory. The real rationalist is one who knows God, the subtlest principle. Mistaking illogic for logic is illogicality. Refuting the rationale of pseudo-rationalists is real rationalism.

Vēdānta is the acme of all epistemological striving, the Truth; it is the reacquisition of one's own inner regions. Sustained efforts to belittle it from time immemorial have not succeeded in veiling its glory.

The wise say, "No one is going to take away anything he has earned in this world," to emphasize the need to transcend mundane thoughts or pursuits. This is often branded "impractical Vēdānta" or dismissed with remarks as "Oh, that is Vēdānta!" by self-styled rationalists.

Although this distorted understanding and misinterpretation might succeed in convincing the uninformed, perhaps temporarily, thus presenting untruth as truth, it cannot veil the truth for long, in the same way that ash cannot conceal live cinder for long; it will remain hidden only until someone blows away the layer of ash to reveal the glowing ember beneath.

Like the wind that blows away the clouds eclipsing the sun, great Masters incarnate from time to time to remove the shroud of ignorance, and thus lay bare the wisdom of the scriptures. History has been witness to this phenomenon. For example, Ācārya Śankara was born at a time when the glory of Sanātana Dharma[41] seemed to come under the threat of rival philosophies, and when the doctrine of Advaita had been relegated to insignificance. In establishing the supremacy of Advaita Vēdānta, he reclaimed the sublime heritage of this holy land.

In today's world, where basic human values such as love and compassion are conspicuous by their absence, we are blessed to have a Master of Amma's stature in our midst to rejuvenate these core values that undeniably sustain our cultural heritage, and to guide us to find happiness within. Our philosophers were not just thinkers; they had transcended thought. The foundation of the philosophy of Bhāratam rests on the experiences of great souls. This is why intellectual analyses by the limited human mind can never grasp the subtlest visionary import enshrined in Vedic philosophy.

When advising Her disciples, Amma would often say, "The import of Amma's words and deeds should be carefully studied and adapted; they contain scriptural truths." She reiterates time and again, "Amma's life is Her message." But often, the subtle appreciation and evaluation of Her

41 'The Eternal Way of Life'; the original and traditional name for Hinduism.

words and deeds require an understanding of the scriptures. The study of scriptures does not automatically lead one to liberation. The knowledge acquired through constant study helps in self-appraisal, which empowers us to remove our impurities. When they are removed, the awareness of the Self dawns. In effect, Self-realization is the very aim of such studies. To those who do not understand the deep import of scriptural works, these texts are merely books.

What I have understood over years of learning about life is that there is always more to learn; not that there is anything to teach. During his last days, Rāmakṛṣṇa Paramahamsa suffered from the agonizing affliction of throat cancer. It is said that a visiting scholar of fame suggested that the Master, being an evolved soul, could easily cure the serious malady by directing the mind in meditative focus to the affected part. The Master's reply was swift: "You're a learned person. You should understand that I have given my mind once and for all to God. How is it then possible to take it back and focus it on this frame of flesh and blood?"

34

Dispelled Doubts

Na kēvalam yō mahatōpabhāṣatē
Śṛṇōti tasmādapi yaḥ sa pāpabhāk
Not only he who speaks ill of the wise but also he who listens to it partakes of sin.

(Kumārasambhavam, 5.83)

There have been many instances of people trying to test Amma's greatness and then being humbled and silenced by Her characteristic simplicity and disarming response. Equal-mindedness and the impartiality arising from it are hallmarks of spiritual greatness. This divine trait has also been eloquently expressed in the Bible thus: "He causes his sun to rise on the evil and the good, and sends rain on the righteous and the unrighteous" (Matthew, 5:43).

A former doubting Thomas, a devotee from Kēraḷa, narrated his experience of Amma's omniscience. About 25 years ago, he heard from his wife about a mahātma, whom she spoke very highly about and greatly adored. She tried to convince him to come and see Amma, but he refused.

He had his own suspicion that this woman whom his wife worshipped was a rank charlatan who hoodwinked the guileless with sleights of hand. But his wife prevailed on him to come to the āśram; she said that he need not go for darśan if he did not wish to. The man agreed, thinking that it would be an opportunity to see firsthand the fraudulence that passed off as faith.

Standing outside the darśan hut, he peered in. Amma was seated at the far end, meeting all those who came to Her. He noticed that some were given more time than others. The cynic in him surmised that the woman probably favored the rich and famous. Right at that very moment, Amma looked up at him, and beckoned him to come near. Startled by this unexpected move, the man hesitated. Amma then said loudly enough for him to hear, "Son, those who are seriously ill need a higher dosage of medicine!" She then resumed giving darśan.

Amma had made Herself crystal clear: that She spent more time with people who were experiencing immense anguish. By singling him out for attention, wasn't She also implying that he needed it, too? How had She read his mind? Although mortified by Amma's words, the man joined the darśan line. Amma received him with much love and affection. Needless to say, the chastened man was won over by Amma's unique medicine, and the erstwhile doubter became a staunch devotee. Maturity is the ability to accept what is true and noble.

A strikingly similar story in the *Śiva Purāṇam*[42] comes to mind. The protagonist of the tale is an extremely devout and spiritually evolved princess, Sīmantinī, the wife of Candrāngada, king of Naiṣadham. An ardent devotee of Śiva and Pārvatī, she underwent severe penance to propitiate them. She spent a lot of time serving devotees of the God and Goddess, especially on Mondays, when she would honor married couples, those who were highly learned and distinguished in scriptural practices, and those established in the service of God. Sīmantinī would offer them valuable gifts in the form of gold ornaments, rich clothing and money as part of her worship (the service intended to support the spiritual and cultural edifice of society).

During this time, two young and learned scholars from Vidarbha, Sumēdhā and Sāmavān, were seeking employment in order to earn adequate wealth to get married and to support their families. Poor by birth, they sought assistance from the king of Vidarbha, who expressed his inability to help but advised them to seek refuge at Sīmantinī's Monday congregation to acquire the intended wealth. But there

42 An ancient collection of narratives about Lord Śiva and His consort Pārvatī, highlighting religious and philosophical concepts, and featuring genealogies of kings, heroes, sages and celestials.

was a catch: only wedded couples were entertained at the worship. The king, who was waiting for an opportunity to assess the depth of Sīmantinī's devotion and spiritual evolution, suggested that the two young men go there disguised as a couple, which meant that one of them would have to play the role of the wife. Reluctantly, they decided to go to Sīmantinī, with Sāmavān dressed up as the young wife. At the service, they were honored and given many presents in the form of gold, gems and silks.

The ploy worked, but they never imagined what a curious victory it would be. On the return journey, Sāmavān found himself changed into a young, well-endowed damsel, shy and markedly graceful in demeanor and speech. Sumēdhā was shocked, to say the least, as were his family and that of Sāmavān. Not knowing how this imbroglio could have befallen them and what remedial measures were available made them all the more upset.

They sought advice from the local ruler who took them to Sage Bharadwāja, who in turn gave them a mantra and instructions on how to invoke Mother Pārvatī by ritualistic penance. After three continuous days of intense worship, the Goddess revealed Herself. Sāmavān beseeched Her to revert him to his original male form, upon which the Goddess expressed Her inability to grant him that wish. Giving an account of the severe and dedicated penance Sīmantinī had undertaken since childhood, She said, "Sīmantinī's austerities have elevated her to formidable levels of spiritual potency, and thus prevents me from granting your wish. Her unflinching devotion compels me to obey her. I am the servant of true devotees." The Goddess, however, offered an alternative to the couple, asking them to remain married, and blessed them with prosperity and happiness.

Even God believers, when they do wrong, practically believe that God is not aware of what they are doing. This belief is essentially sheer ignorance and a lack of faith. If only man would utilize one fourth of the energy he fritters away in perpetrating his ignorance, for seeking God!

This narrative also highlights the power and intensity of the spiritual will of evolved individuals, even though fools consider such will power unimportant because it is deficient in them. "*Sankalpanam hi sankalpaḥ*,"—"Indeed, making a strong resolution is *sankalpa*" (*Yōgavāsiṣṭham*).

A profound verse from a song, which I had the privilege of scoring and singing, comes to mind:

> *Ceytatinotta phalam nukarumbōḷ ciri tūkum cilar kara-yum*
>
> While experiencing the fruits of action, some smile in joy and some weep in sorrow.
>
> (from '*Kālam kanalu pozhikkunnu*')

This verse was written by Swāmi Turīyāmṛtānanda Puri, one of the senior monks of Amma's order. I have had the good fortune of scoring many of the songs he has written, such as '*Arivāy amṛtāy*' and '*Varunnennu tōnnunnu.*'

35

Master Musician

There were times during Dēvī Bhāva when Amma would thrust the sword toward a devotee playing an instrument, when a momentary lapse in concentration would make him miss a beat and compromise the rhythm. But Amma's absolute control and poise was revealed by the fact that no one was ever injured in this process.

An incident that happened some time later is indicative of Amma's emphasis on the perfection we should strive to reproduce in music. I used to play the *mṛdangam*,[43] *tabla* and

43 Barrel-shaped, double-headed drum, considered to be the most ancient of drums. Amma has said that the sound of the tamburu, vīṇā (the Indian lute associated with Goddess Saraswatī), flute and mṛdangam can be heard in deep contemplation.

dhōlak for the bhajan group. Missing a beat on one occasion and fearing a thrust of Amma's sword, I threw the dhōlak into Br. Bālagōpāl's lap in a moment of childish fear. This incident became the butt of jokes for a long time. Amma would often recount it in Her inimitable style.

Br. Nīlu (now Swāmi Paramātmānanda Puri) used to play the harmonium during the Kṛṣṇa Bhāva, in spite of all his physical infirmities. During Amma's bhajans, it was Br. Srīkumār (now Swāmi Pūrṇāmṛtānanda Puri) who played the harmonium. I enjoyed playing the percussion instruments with both of them, such was the natural rapport between us. I look back with much nostalgia on those days when I would also sing in total abandon while playing the tabla, for long hours during the bhāva darśans, absorbed in thoughts of Amma, and never wondering what others thought about my singing.

In those days, I used to tune the *tamburu*[44] and give it to Amma, who would sit with it almost every morning, gently plucking the strings and losing Herself in its sweet, meditative drone. Amma's demeanor—as She sat with eyes closed, the tamburu's gourd resting on Her lap, and Her slender fingers picking successively at each of the strings—was regal, saintly and divine all at the same time.

---

44 Instrument that resembles a lute and is used as a drone accompaniment.

Amma's empathy for music and musical instruments is keen. Once, She unexpectedly walked into a room in which I used to store various musical instruments, including the tamburu, percussion instruments and the harmonium. She started tapping some of the tablas and mṛdangams, and stopped when She heard one or two that were not in tune. Amma then turned to me and said that the instruments had to be kept tuned 24 hours a day. In a serious tone, Amma explained that musical instruments were to be regarded as manifestations of Saraswatī Herself, the Goddess of Learning and the Arts, and that one would incur sin if these instruments were left unattended to.

Once, during Amma's bhajans, I started hitting the sides of the tabla a little too hard with the hammer in order to tune it and bring it to the pitch in which Amma was going to sing the next bhajan. She turned around and asked me to be gentler; Amma said that the tabla has life in it, and that I was hurting it by hitting it so hard.

A few years after I joined the āśram, I was presented with a 200-year-old mṛdangam that had once belonged to a renowned mṛdangist. It was a rare gift and I took very good care of it. When played well, the mṛdangam would create tones of indescribable resonance and brightness. Many people asked me for it; some even offered to pay high sums. Once, a very famous percussionist approached me and offered to pay thousands of rupees for the mṛdangam. It was a huge amount at that time. I went to Amma and told Her about the offer. She immediately said that I should not part with it; Amma explained that its *kutti*—the main, wooden, barrel-shaped body of the instrument—was ancient, and that no one alive knew the art of making such perfect kuttis anymore. Such was Amma's rapport with musical instruments. I realized that it was not just people but also seemingly inanimate objects of which Amma had intimate knowledge.

Her own command and mastery of music are so immense as to be unfathomable. Once, a classical singer of high repute and devotee of Amma reported how she had sung a composition in the Ārabhi *rāga* (melodic pattern) during a concert. She had begun the rendition with an elaborate *ālāp* (freewheeling, improvised overture), during which time she had taken pains to highlight subtle nuances of the rāga's texture. At one point during the elaboration, she wondered for a moment if what she had executed was orthodox, or if she had deviated ever so slightly from tradition. However, this was just one moment in a very long piece. At its conclusion, she felt that she had sung the composition well. No one seemed to have noticed any aberration in her singing. Not only that, the renowned singers and musicologists in attendance congratulated her for the command performance.

That night, she had a dream in which Amma congratulated her on having expressed the rāga well, and then pointed out how she had erred a little during the middle portion of the ālāp. Amma then sang that part to let her hear how she could have sung that phrase; it was precisely the section where she had wondered if the rāga had been rendered inaccurately.

Once, a few famous artists from AIR (All-India Radio) came to the āśram for a recording of Amma's bhajans. At the end of the recording, some of them, who were renowned for both their knowledge of music as well as their compositions, commented on Amma's *svara śuddhi*, i.e. the purity of voice. They said that in their many years of working with outstanding musicians, they had met many gifted singers but that there was something in the timbre of Amma's voice that they had not heard anywhere else: for want of better words, they called it soulful purity.

I have been complimented for my singing as well as my compositions. With all honesty and humility, I can say that the modest wealth in my musical outpourings has been gleaned from Amma. Whether it is svara śuddhi, *śruti* (pitch) or *bhāva* (mood), my firm opinion is that Amma is unrivalled. After years of listening to Amma singing, I have come to the conclusion that music should transcend the level of the physical; it should reduce our desires, not increase them. It should melt the heart of the audience and performer alike. When Amma sings, She cries and makes others cry as well.

Often, I think She is not just the Muse but Music itself.

36

Midnight Melody

Once, during Amma's 2010 US Tour, my telephone at the Pālakkaṭ āśram rang after midnight, unusual for that late hour. Putting my work aside, I picked up the receiver. It was Amma, speaking during the drive from one of the centers to another. My foremost thought was how to initiate a conversation with Her. Would the customary "How are You, Ammē?" do? Would that greeting be appropriate with this great Master, who transcends all limits of the human senses? Would the informal approach that comes to me naturally in my interactions with Amma do, or should it be more formal? Struggling inwardly to find an apt way to begin a dialogue, I remained breathlessly tongue-tied for some time.

Under normal circumstances, an inquiry such as "*Sukhamāṇō?*" ("Are you well?") reflects the genuine interest in the welfare and happiness of the person to whom we are speaking. However, when we are aware that the person is the embodiment of Bliss, what sense or propriety is there in asking, "Sukhamāṇō?"

As if understanding my predicament, Amma took the initiative and asked, "Son, are you well?"

Part nervously and somewhat excitedly, I responded briefly: "*Sukamāṇammē*" ("I am well, Amma").

Telephone calls from Amma are neither rare nor new to me since there have been numerous occasions in the past when She called from Amṛtapuri and other locations. I have had many opportunities to travel abroad with Amma. But this was one of those times when I had not accompanied Her, and so, there was a touch of anxiousness and excitement in my answer.

Following my response, there was silence, a long lingering one, made all the more charged by the unusually silent setting of the night, and by the awareness that the caller was none other than the Master Herself speaking from across the world. "Show me someone who has lost the power of words. I want to speak to him," said a Zen Master, hinting at the divine potency of silence. Noteworthy is this mantra "*Ōm niśśabda jananīgarbha nirgamādbhuta karmaṇē namaḥ*" (24)

("Obeisance to Amma, who performed the astonishing feat of coming out of the mother's womb silently") from Amma's *Aṣṭōttaraśatanāmāvali* (108 attributes of Śrī Mātā Amṛtānandamayī Dēvī) composed by Ōṭṭūr Uṇṇi Nanpūtirippāṭ.

Amma continued on the phone, "Son, I was thinking of you," and what followed was music divine. She started crooning one of my favorite bhajans, which I had earlier scored and sung with Amma, '*Manassoru māyā marīcika.*' As She sang the entire song over several minutes, I felt that I was being subjected to Amma's singular, loving attention from across the globe, an unparalleled treat! More remarkable was Amma's special efforts to emphasize the nuances I would take pains to express in the ascending and descending notes during singing.

This naturally made me ask, "Amma, do you think my nature to delve into the subtler aspects of music while singing is consistent with my spiritual path?"

Amma's reply was delectably reassuring. "Son, music is inherent in you; it will instinctively surface in your singing. Pure, soulful music surpasses even bhakti."

"After silence, that which comes nearest to expressing the inexpressible is Music." Aldous Huxley once remarked.

My childish delight got a shot in the arm when, following this, Amma also told me that She had mimicked the mannerisms I usually exhibit when settling down to lead a music program. I later learned from devotees who had been present with Amma and had gleefully enjoyed Her performance, that She had made the scene extremely hilarious. Announcing that She was being 'Praṇavāmṛta' at the moment, to the delight of everyone there, Amma imitated my sitting pose, complete with my usual gestures of spreading a small Turkish towel on the lap and a neatly folded shawl over the shoulder. She mimicked my habit of stroking the folds gently while attempting to adjust them carefully to ensure a consummately aesthetic look.

Once, when I accompanied Amma to Europe, I overheard Her telling a few devotees in Amsterdam, "In music, Praṇavāmṛta can soar like a bird." On another occasion, Amma said, "If he heard the buzz of a mosquito, he would start humming in that very pitch!"

It was Her affection that made Amma speak so highly of me. As far as I am concerned, I am not a great singer at all. In fact, I feel that I have never sung in my life—to really sing is to sing for God and God alone, the way Amma does, forgetting everything else. Will I ever be able to sing soulfully?

The great poet Kāḷidāsa, in his immortal work '*Kumārasambhavam*,' sings, "*Kim punarbrahmayōnēryastava cētasi vartatē*," (6.18) meaning, "The one You (God) recall is the most blessed of the blessed!"

There is enough space for all us in Amma's heart, which is as expansive as the sky. She once told me, "Before I sleep, I go to each one of you individually, and give you my loving hugs and kisses." Indeed, all of us who are living in this age with Amma are truly blessed.

na hi jñānēna sadṛśam pavitramiha vidyatē
tatsvayam yōgasamsiddhaḥ kālēnātmani vindati
Verily there exists nothing as purifying in this world as knowledge. In good time, having purified the mind and becoming established in Yoga, one realizes the Self in one's own heart.

(*Bhagavad Gītā*, 4.38)

Part Five

Auspiciousness

37

Enshrined Ethos

The ambience of the kaḷari had a striking likeness to the vibrations that prevailed in my ancestral house during festivities associated with the family deity (Dēvī of Cheṭṭikuḷangara Bhagavatī Temple), who was, in Her subtle aspect, Amma Herself. The temple shrine and its presiding deity contributed greatly to my joining Amma's fold, not least because of the striking similarity in the features of both, and because of Amma's presence and participation in the festivities in earlier years. She had taken part in the renowned *'Kuttiyōṭṭam'* festival associated with this Bhagavatī temple. Incidentally, Amma's first-ever public program was held in this temple.

The local Dēvī shrine is an ancient temple situated in Māvēlikkara. It is of enormous significance to my pre-monastic family, since this Goddess had been the family deity from ancient days. The relevance of such shrines dates back to the earliest of times. It is believed that regions like Māvēlikkara were divided into several zones, each connected to a specific place of worship consecrated for the purpose. The prosperity and well-being of the people and their homes in a particular zone were associated with the deity of the temple in that locality. Thus, the deity of these shrines, worshipped over generations, came to be regarded as the family deity. Such shrines of worship are highly venerated, and devotees take great pains to ensure that people participate in and contribute to the annual festival associated with these shrines.

Summer is the time of festivities for people here, as it generally is all over Kērāḷa. The annual festival of this Bhagavatī Temple is known as '*Kumbhabharaṇi*,' hailed as one among the greatest events in Kērāḷa. It is celebrated with pomp and pageantry. Hundreds of thousands of people from various regions in Kērāḷa and outside descend on Cheṭṭikuḷangara for this mega-event.

The highlights of the Kumbhabharaṇi festival are '*Kuttiyōṭṭam*' and '*Keṭṭukāzhca*,' the principal offerings to the presiding Goddess. The Kuttiyōṭṭam starts about a week before the rise of the *Bharaṇi* star. The first day of the festival coincides with *Śivarātri*.[45]

Śivarātri is the Auspicious Night; Śiva is not an individual but stands for the principle of auspiciousness. Devotees generally observe the event by keeping an all-night vigil spent in prayers.

Once, when Amma was lying down with eyes closed, presumably taking a nap, I asked Her (when She opened Her eyes), "Amma, were You sleeping?"

Amma's reply was spontaneous: "Child, there is no sleep for Amma, only eternal vigilance. Amma is always in the state of a witness."

Whereas the Kuttiyōṭṭam is generally conducted by individual devotees and family units, Keṭṭukāzhca is open to the 13 zones (*karas*) that come under the purview of the temple. Each of the zones presents its offering as one united community. The Kumbhabharaṇi is followed by a 13-day temple festival conducted by the 13 karas.

Amma would remind us that shrines and associated festivals have their roots in the days of yore, and that they were regarded as an important part of the social order because they instill righteousness in people, thus preventing them from falling prey to temptations, which in turn results in the erosion of the value system. "*Dharmō rakṣati rakṣitaḥ*" ("He

45 Literally, 'Night of Śiva.' The dark night in the lunar calendar, the 14th phase of the waning moon culminating in the new moon in the 'Phālguṇa' month.

who protects Dharma is, in turn, protected by it") declares the *Manusmṛti* (8.15).

The idols in these temples were consecrated in olden times by great sages who wielded immense spiritual power gained through years of penance. Consequently, these idols are not merely sculpted stones. They are shrines enlivened by the intense spiritual energy that has been infused into them. These sanctums are thus a major source of energy for devotees, giving them relief and succor.

For devotees, the Goddess was not just an idol, but a living reality to whom they had grown so close that it was commonplace for many of them to say, "I will be gone for a little while. I will call on *Vallyamma*[46] and return soon!" Invariably, the temples had ponds, rare herbal and shady trees, as well as reptiles and other animals associated with the temples in one way or the other. Citing this, Amma would explain how these centers of worship had promoted environmental protection over the centuries.

The week-long Kuttiyōṭṭam revelry features the worship of the Goddess in the form of 'Bhadrakāḷī.'[47] The stage upon which the Goddess was seated would be adorned with

46 *A term of endearment showing respect to an elderly female family member.*
47 *'Bhadram Kalayatīti Bhadrakāḷī' ('One who causes auspiciousness'); the ferocious form of the Goddess.*

captivating floral decorations, with blooms of various hues and scents. Lit bronze lamps of various shapes and sizes would conjure the aura of sanctity that is so unique to such settings. Beats from a combination of drums would give a rhythmic boost to the folk songs sung on such evenings.

Massive shelters, propped on wholesome betel-nut log scaffolding, reinforced with bamboo roofing and artfully thatched with coconut leaves, for large-scale communal feeding on all the seven days of the event are a common sight at the program venue. The scale and sophistication of the infrastructure and decorations for this mega-event reflected the social status and affluence of the family groups staging the spectacle.

Amma took part in the historic Kuttiyōṭṭam when She was specially invited by a devotee to honor his home with Her divine presence during the festival. A large crowd of family members and their relatives, participants from the neighboring localities, and visiting members from outside had already gathered when Amma and the group accompanying Her, consisting of both Indian and foreign devotees, arrived. I was also privileged to be a part of this occasion. Amma's appearance roused the inspired crowd who had been engrossed in the '*Kuttiyōṭṭaccuvaṭukaḷ*' (rhythmic movement of the feet) performed by experts. Caught in the wave of excitement, a few of Amma's Western children lost no time in picking up the dance steps, prancing about to the rhythm, and blending in with the other performers.

38

Manifold Magnificence

The scene brought back nostalgic memories of my childhood when, year after year, the occasion used to thrill me with its multi-faceted magnificence. I recalled the two occasions when I was part of the Kuttiyōṭṭam hosted by my ancestral (maternal) family, as well as the elders' account of the event before I was born.

'Parayeṭuppu' and *'Jīvata' Ezhunnaḷḷattu* (procession) are rituals peculiar to regions like Māvēlikkara. The word 'jīvata' implies that the consciousness of the temple deity (Mother Goddess) has been invoked. A symbolic art form, Jīvata is a blend of architecture and expert craftsmanship, a precisely measured simulacrum of the shrine itself. A box-like carriage for the deity rests on wooden poles. It resembles a palanquin, its front representing the deity. This is central to the Parayeṭuppu activity.

The Jīvata pageant, visiting the houses of devotees, is unique in its character and form. The procession consisted of temple employees playing percussion instruments and carrying lamps and the pedestal for the Goddess. As it is about to commence its move from the temple premises, fire-crackers are set off to announce the deity's approach to the locality, and residents hurry to make last-minute touches to the reception they have prepared for the Mother Goddess.

The Jīvata, shoulder-borne by two priests, moves at a very swift pace set to *Ceṇṭa*[48] beats on its run from the temple, the priest in front powering his way ahead in graceful strides, and the priest behind matching the pace. It is said that the amazing speed at which the two move with the heavy structure on their shoulders cannot be attributed to the brawn of the priests but to the very presence of the Divine Mother Herself.

Once it enters a household, the bearers put the Jīvata down gently and reverently on a pedestal, brought from the temple for this purpose, right in front of the house, enabling the family members to worship and submit their offerings. The Jīvata's presence would often give rise to a high-octane display of emotional cries from the devout who seem to become possessed by the divine, leading to euphoric expressions of joy and revelry.

48 A South Indian drum

Drums and other musical instruments are then played, and devotees join the visiting group to express their happiness. The priests then hoist the Jīvata onto their shoulders, and the leading member moves back and forth, sideways and in circles, all in graceful steps, balancing it delicately, the one behind amazingly matching the steps of the priest in front. The attendant devotee crowd, in raptures, is moved to emotional outbursts of cries such as "*Ammē! Dēvī! Mahāmāyē!*" the roaring sounds rising heavenwards in a crescendo, expressing their sense of fulfillment.

The conduct and festivities associated with the 'Parayeṭuppu' had captivated my imagination as a young boy so much that I had insisted on getting a replica of the 'Godhead' that the priests used to carry on their shoulders during their house visits. My aunt, her husband and her mother (my grandmother) were indulgent and, relenting to my demand, arranged for a miniature wooden replica of the Jīvata. I used to revel in carrying this small Jīvata and, accompanied by my friends, visiting the neighboring houses, getting emotionally charged during the play-acting.

The vast influence that the Goddess of the local shrine exercised on the people of the region was instrumental in sustaining their sense of righteousness and morality, a culture that has been handed down from generation to generation. If there was open admiration and deference that the presence of the deity evoked, there was also an unmistakable element of fear and apprehension that wrong-doers would receive serious chastisement should they upset the social order and peace of the people in the region. When I was in college, whenever circumstances and peers tempted me to do wrong, the image of Cheṭṭikuḷangara Dēvī would come to mind, and I would refrain from doing wrong out of *bhaya-bhakti*, devotion inspired by fear of repercussion.

One of the most popular and dynamic forms of the Universal Mother, Bhadrakāḷī is invincible, regarded as the fierce yet compassionate, demon-slaying protector of the devout and righteous. Possessing a radiantly dark complexion, She is generally depicted as a four-armed Goddess. Her terrible form instills mortal fear in the wicked, who perpetrate vice and undermine the security and peace of society.

Among the many saints and seekers who achieved liberation through the worship of Mother Kāḷī, the most well-known is Śrī Rāmakṛṣṇa Paramahamsa, who had this to say:

My Mother is the principle of consciousness. She is *Akhaṇḍa Saccidānanda*—the indivisible Existence, Knowledge, Bliss absolute. The night sky between the stars is perfectly black. The waters of the ocean depths are the same; the infinite is always mysteriously dark. This inebriating darkness is my beloved Kāḷī.

"*Tēbhyō haitadakṣaramuvāca da iti*" expounds the *Bṛhadāraṇyakōpaniṣad* (5.2.1). When *dēvas* (celestial beings), humans and *asuras* (demons) sought spiritual guidance from Prajāpati,[49] the latter uttered the syllable *'Da.'* The pleasure loving Dēvas construed it as *'Dama,'* meaning abstinence, the human beings interpreted it to mean *'Dānam,'* meaning charity, and the asuras took it as *'Daya,'* or compassion. These three values are instilled in the masses through temple culture.

49 1. God presiding over creation; 2. an epithet of Brahmā, the Creator; 3. any one of the 10 ṛṣis created by Brahmā at the beginning of the creation.

39

Striking Similarity

The close similarity between the Dēvī in the shrine and Amma could not be attributed to mere coincidence. The emotional cries hailing the Goddess during the Bharaṇi festival were just like the soulful cries of "*Ammā! Ammachī! Dēvī! Bhagavatī! Mahāmāyē!*" that greeted Amma during Dēvī Bhāva.

Another occasion when I noticed a parallel between the two divinities was when the team of performers who sing and dance in the Kuttiyōṭṭam visited Amma to seek Her blessings. Their visit proved to be a highlight of Amma's Dēvī manifestation that day. The Kuttiyōṭṭam team embarked on a series of dynamic songs, one after the other, without a break between the ending of one and the beginning of the next. The full-throated, vigorous singing to pulsating beats from a host of percussion instruments set a swift pace for Amṛtā Dēvī's nṛtta. Amma would dance spiritedly, and for much longer than usual, filling the hearts of Her children with soulful joy.

The demeanor of the temple team suggested that the performers saw Amma as no different from the Goddess of the shrine, and that this was, for them, a family reunion, children joyfully reuniting with their mother. The way the group members engaged with Amma during darśan also revealed an endearing mother-child relation.

I recalled the exhilarating dreams I used to have recurrently during my childhood. I would see visions of a reassuringly benign and captivating female form, Dēvī, who would have a sword in one hand and a trident in the other. The form would bless me, and on one occasion, She also gave me a mantra to chant. The form would later dance, captivating my inner senses. I would neither become disturbed nor unduly perplexed, although I did wonder what its relevance was. The dream repeated several times until I saw Amma's Dēvī Manifestation, the arresting similarity between the 'real' and 'dream' versions revealing the providential significance of the visions. Having discovered the unity of Dēvī and Amma, I could see also the subtle connection to my abounding faith in and devotion to the '*paradēvata*' (family deity).

On the one hand, the deep bonding with my iṣṭa dēvata Kṛṣṇa—synonym of beauty, intelligence, skill and equipoise, and role model in every part he played—was total and unequivocal. On the other, enshrined in the recesses of my heart was the Mother Goddess of the temple, cherished by Her devotees as unfailing protector and guardian of dharma. The fact was that I thought of myself primarily as a Kṛṣṇa devotee, notwithstanding my association with the local Dēvī shrine. The repetitive dream revealed that I had an abiding faith in the Goddess.

That day, when the enigma of those dreams was resolved, I realized that the benign angel of my dreams had manifested because of my deep-rooted devotion to my paradēvata. Not only that, I was left without a trace of doubt that Amṛtā Dēvī and the paradēvata were one and the same.

40

Enchanting Energy

"Numberless are the world's wonders, but none more wonderful than man," observed Sophocles. The creation of the phenomenal universe does not involve only matter and energy but the will as well. Thus the inspiration for creation is Dēvī, the Universal Mother, who has to be invoked in the individual soul's quest for finding its roots and unity in the Divine, the conscious identifying itself as the super-conscious.

The ancient epic, *Rāmāyaṇa*, provides an unambiguous explication of this subtle point. The three principal protagonists in this story are symbolic of the three factors that characterize creation: Paramātma, Māyā and the Jīvātma. They are depicted thus: Rāma in the lead, Sītā close behind, and Lakṣmaṇa trailing behind Sītā, a figurative suggestion of Māyā veiling the Jīvātma's path to supreme consciousness. In order to reach its objective (Rāma, symbolizing the Paramātma), the Jīvātma (Lakṣmaṇa) has to earnestly invoke the grace and blessings of Dēvī (Māyā, characterized by Sītā), who alone can grant the wish; no other strategy borne either of logic or rationale can liberate the Jīvātma in distress. Lakṣmaṇa cannot command Sītā to move away so that he can gain direct access to Rāma; She must deign to move.

The web of delusion can blind and deceive the Jīvātma, confining it in a world of fantasy for infinite lives. The *Yōgavāsiṣṭham* is lucid on this point:

> *Ahō vicitrāmāyēyam bata viśvavimōhinī*
>
> Lo! How strange and wondrous is this world-bewitching Māyā, the grand illusion!

Amma uses the analogy of threading the needle. If the thread is thick, uneven or rough, it cannot be pushed through the eye of the needle; the thread has to be compacted so that it can pass through the needle, symbolizing surrender to its final aim of being able to stitch the cloth. Likewise, surrender in its broadest and most subtle sense—to submit oneself wholly and unconditionally at the lotus feet of the Guru—is the means for the success of the individual self (Jīvātma) in realizing and attaining the Supreme Self (Paramātma).

Therefore, a seeker of Truth has to continuously and fervently invoke the Universal Mother for Her blessings to guide him at each and every step of the way to the ultimate goal.

My conviction, rooted in personal observation and experience, is that through illusion, the Universal Mother limits the vision and path of the individual soul to realization, and consequently, Her blessings are essential to reach the goal. She is *Māyā* (power of illusion) but also *Māyātītā* (one who transcends the illusory state). I recall the captivating Carṇātic (South Indian classical) composition in the Māyāmāḷavagauḷa rāga: '*Māyātītasvarūpiṇi*' ('O Universal Mother, whose nature transcends the power of illusion').

In effect, the importance of the Universal Mother has to be understood to enable the seeker to progress on the spiritual path. Dēvī is both the means and the end; Her divine form is the means, and the Absolute Principle She stands for is the end. She has to be the focus of the fervent seeker in his march towards eventual liberation. She alone, who is no different from the highest truth, is Māyā. Also, the statement "*Yā mā sā Māyā*" means "That which is not is Māyā." When the veil of Māyā is removed, the realization that "*Sarvam khalvidam Brahma*"—"All this (universe) is indeed Brahman"—(*Chāndōgyōpaniṣad*, 3.14.1) dawns, which again requires the blessings of Mahāmāyā, the Universal Mother!

The *Mahābhārata* is emphatic in its pronouncement,

Nāsti mātṛsamā chāyā nāsti mātṛsamā gatiḥ
Nāsti mātṛsamam trāṇam nāsti mātṛsamā priyā

> There is none like the mother in providing us with protection, refuge, safety and love.
>
> *(Mahābhārata, 12.265.31)*

A valid question that might crop up is, "Aren't there instances of souls who attained deliverance by worshipping other deities such as Śiva, Viṣṇu, Kṛṣṇa, Gaṇēśa and Kārtikēya?" While this cannot be denied, my contention is that the power to overcome the factors that veil the transcendence is essentially attributable to the underlying Will, or Śakti (the Dēvī element), of any aspect of divinity. I have become immensely convinced of this over the past 33 years of my association with Amma.

Ācārya Śankara in *Saundarya Laharī* expresses the idea thus:

> *Śivaśaktyā yuktō yadi bhavati śaktaḥ prabhavitum*
> Even Lord Śiva is capable of action only if and when He is united with Śakti, the Primordial Energy. (1)

This is high praise indeed for Dēvī but for whose Will, Śiva the Supreme would not have been able to express anything on His own!

I realized the truth that there was no alternative to invoking Dēvī's grace for mental equipoise, the key to ensuring success. Guru Nānak says, "The light which is in everything is Thine, O Lord of Light. From its brilliancy everything is brilliant; by the Guru's teaching, the light becomes manifest."

An analogy that explains the connotation of the term 'Māyā' is that of a rope appearing to be a snake in the dark. The rope is the reality and the snake is an illusion. Whereas the stated example brings forth the inter-relation of the cause and effect, the universe of time and space projects itself as reality to our limited intelligence, akin to the snake in the example.

Just as a dreamer awakens into the wakeful state, the Jīvātma, hitherto clouded in ignorance, becomes increasingly aware of higher orders of reality as he progresses spiritually. This phenomenal world that we behold is only relatively true whereas God is absolutely real. Māyā is the inscrutable power that superimposes the changing universe of names and forms on the changeless Absolute reality. Plato summed it up when he said, "You cannot conceive of the many without the One." Amma reiterates the point, "Creation and the creator are not two but one." Anyone who has heard Her soulful rendering of the bhajan '*Sṛṣṭiyum nīyē srasṭāvum nīyē*' would not have missed the point!

The physical, mental and moral conditions that straitjacket the individual soul cause limitations, preventing it from discerning the reality of the Divine. In Ramaṇa Maharṣi's words, "Mind is consciousness that has put on limitations.

You are originally unlimited and perfect. Later, you take on limitations and become the mind."

41

Egoless Existence

Some years ago, a drunkard who had mended his ways after meeting Amma came to see Her in Amṛtapuri. During darśan, She reassured him with the words, "Son, don't worry. Amma is always with you."

The man replied, "That's precisely my problem, Amma, that You are always with me! I can't even buy a can of beer! Every time I try, I see You before me!"

To a Master, everything is an open book. There are no secrets hidden from them, but they conceal their omniscience most of the time in their natural modesty. Many years ago, during a Dēvī Bhāva, a Western woman who had just had darśan came out of the kaḷari looking stunned. She saw me and headed straight towards me. She asked frantically, "You... English?"

I figured that what she meant was whether I knew English. I asked her to tell me what she wanted. Pointing to the kaḷari, she gasped, "Amma... French!"

Amma had obviously spoken to her in French. This incident occurred at a time when Amma had not started going for Her world tours, and Western devotees were a very rare sight in the āśram. How had Amma, who had hardly ever stepped out of this humble fishing village nestled in a nook of Kēraḷa, come upon this knowledge?

I recall the time when Amma invited some of the female āśram residents and devotees present to lift Her off the ground. A few of them tried, but failed. They tried again and again, but failed each time. Just as they were about to give up, Amma prevailed on them to make one final attempt. Lo! They had hardly put their hands together, and Amma appeared to levitate as if on Her own, becoming considerably lighter to the group.

In this context, I also remember Amma, who used to be lean and slender, often telling us that She would gain weight in time to become plump and rotund, in order to assume a typical maternal look.

The Sānskṛt root of the word 'Dēvī' is '*div*,' which means to shine. Amma is hailed as 'Śrī Mātā Amṛtānandamayī Dēvī' because She is verily the consciousness that shines in all beings. That is why She knows all the thoughts and feelings that pass through our minds. The all-knowingness of mahātmas can also be explained by the fact that they do not identify with their limiting adjuncts, which bind us and cause ignorance. Our ego, which we wear like a badge of honor, actually constricts our outlook. It betrays itself in utterances such as "I think it was in 1991 that Amma saw *me* for the first time!"

Fortunately for us, Amma knows our limitations and is ever patient with us. There was a devotee who had sat for an examination, for which she was hoping to do well. However, her anxiety about how she had performed made her think that she might not do so well after all. She lowered her expectation, hoping to score at least 60%. Soon, that thought became an obsession. She would look up at the sky and see the clouds in the shape of a '6,' regarding this as an omen, a sign from God that she would pass with 60%. While combing her hair, she would predetermine thus: "If the hair I shed falls on the floor and forms the shape of '6,' I know that I will pass with at least 60%." In this and other ways, the girl began obsessing over the outcome of the exams.

During this time, she went to Amṛtapuri for Amma's darśan. When her turn came, Amma asked her, "So, have you finished fantasizing about seeing sixes everywhere?"

The girl was taken aback by Amma's pointed awareness of her fixation, for she had not told anyone about it. Moments later, Amma laughingly consoled the devotee and assured her that she would pass well. When the results were released, the girl learned that she had scored more than 70%.

Spiritual masters, whose minds are untinged by even the faintest trace of egoism, do not identify with their body; theirs is a cosmic consciousness. There is a story of a well-known avadhūtā who was always surrounded by a pack of dogs. Once, the avadhūtā sustained a wound on her leg that did not heal. After some time, whiffing the tang of blood, the dogs started licking it. The taste of blood whetted their appetite for flesh, and soon, the dogs started biting into the avadhūtā's leg. Horrified by the sight, some devotees started beating the dogs and chasing them away. Much to their astonishment, the avadhūtā beat and berated *them* for harassing the dogs. Such was the saint's freedom from bodily identification and empathy for all beings.

When restrictions disappear, the individual soul (Jīvātma) merges with the universal spirit (Paramātma), bringing forth the realization of the ultimate unity of existence. Whereas the sight of a tiny spider-web motivates an observer to look for its architect (the spider), this universe—with its endless mysteries, inscrutable wonders, and dimensionless marvels in time and space that continue to confound man—does not seem to spur him to seek its source, to look for its creator. If this is not evidence of Māyā's mesmerizing might, what is?

Amma says, "Children, just as you endeavor to meditate with closed eyes, you should try to do so with open eyes, too."

This is a gem of an advice for everyone. Irrespective of the action performed, the mind has to be trained to focus inwards. In short, karma should not remain confined to its fundamental connotation of action; it ought to become a medium of contemplation.

Karma does not purport to liberate a jīva from the clutches of ignorance; the jīva is freed only through wisdom arising from transcendental meditation. More than anything else, the aspirant should be single-minded in his search of the indwelling spirit. Actions performed with a pure and unselfish attitude of surrender help one overcome mental aberrations. This then facilitates the progression to deep meditation, which in turn leads to knowledge of the Self, the stepping-stone to final liberation.

Whereas the scientist's sphere of work is the laboratory wherein he arrives at rational and logical inferences, the ṛṣi's domain of research was the inner laboratory of Self-analysis where he sought to unravel mysteries beyond the ken of reason. Just as a scientist resolves to discover facts pertaining to the subject of his study in the external world of details, the inspired seer explores the mystery of creation and his own Self in the inner realm of spirit.

In spite of all its limitations, the human mind can succeed in this quest; its success hinges on pure *śraddha* (attentiveness), which leads to transcendence, eventually taking one to supreme bliss. Forging ahead on the wings of a chaste and sublime mind borne by spiritual enthusiasm, the seeker soars on this state of awareness to attain illumination.

42

Sublime Sagacity

The King of Syracuse, Hieron, had a close friend in the celebrated Greek thinker, Simonides. Once, the king asked his friend, "Can you tell me what God is?"

Simonides reflected for a few moments and then said, "Sire, give me two days and I will have the answer for you."

At the end of the two days, when the king inquired about the answer, Simonides requested that he be given three more days. At the end of those three days, Simonides wanted another four days. Annoyed at this, the king demanded an explanation for the continued delay.

"Ah, My Lord," replied Simonides, "You ask what God is. But the more I reflect on that sublime subject, the less I understand it! God is a mystery that cannot be explained!"

If one does not know oneself, then what is the point of knowing anything else? If one knows the Self, then he knows everything.

A couple of lines from a bhajan that Amma sings, insinuating themselves into my mind, reassured me of the understanding I had gained that evening: "*Sūcanakaḷ nalkīṭām ñān ētonnāṇī poruḷennu mānasamē uṇarnnu nī ariññukoḷka*"—"I shall give you hints about the nature of this truth. Wake up, O mind, to know what it is."

According to tradition, the spiritual path emphasizes the spirit of inquiry, requiring the seeker to look within. Facilitating this search is the Guru's grace. Thus the Guru (one's own discriminative intellect) is portrayed in this bhajan as the one who gives hints or, in other words, shows the path.

"A nation's culture resides in the hearts and in the soul of its people," said Gāndhiji. India's cultural heritage is most ancient, several thousand years old. Such is the strength of its social and religious structure that it has withstood the invasions and persecutions that have occurred at regular intervals over the millennia. Paying tribute to the richness of this culture, former Indian President Dr. Abdul Kalam remarked, "We have not invaded anyone. We have not conquered anyone. We have not grabbed anyone's land... and tried to enforce our way of life on anyone."

Unique in its diversity of physical, religious, racial, linguistic and artistic dispositions, the eternal values, imparted by ancient sages and mystics of the highest truth who lived and remained wedded to the loftiest levels of spiritual life, have helped unify the myriad facets of this rich and unparalleled culture, like a thread in a garland of fresh and fragrant flowers.

Life in ancient times was regulated by customs and practices bequeathed by great sages and visionaries who viewed them as an indispensable part of life. Emphasis was on strengthening the mental attitude, which enriched peace and harmony for the people. Religion is a way of life in India.

During an overseas visit, Amma was asked, "Why is it that greats like Rāma, Kṛṣṇa and Amma are born in India?"

Amma answered, "Children, we are required to pour water at the roots of the tree. The water poured at the roots will naturally spread to all parts. The root of spiritual learning is Bhāratam (India)."

India is a country that has always held knowledge in the highest regard. Once, a visitor asked Amma, "What is the proof that the Vēdas belong to Bhāratam?"

'*Vēda*' essentially means 'Supreme Knowledge,' even though it is generally taken to refer to particular scriptural texts, *viz.* the *Ṛg*, *Yajus*, *Sāma* and *Atharva* Vēdas. It follows then that anyone who embodies this wisdom is a carrier of the Vēdas, the Supreme Knowledge. The wise are not restricted to any one geographical location. However, the questioner's interest seems to be in the physical provenance of this wisdom. While questions are encouraged in Sanātana Dharma—as is evident from several Upaniṣads and a few other scriptural texts, which are in a question-and-answer format—it is incumbent upon the questioner (seeker) to ask with the proper attitudes, i.e. humility and *jijñāsā* (eagerness to know). For one thing, the question was being put to Amma, the personification of the Vēdas, who is from Bhāratam, as were the seers who bequeathed the Vēdas to humanity. For another, when one obtains the blessing of being able to ask questions or clear doubts with someone of Amma's stature, one should utilize the opportunity to pose questions that will dispel the fogginess that clouds our perception of the Truth instead of making insinuations.

It is imperative that only those who have a clear vision of the spiritual objective can guide or lead seekers on that path. One who has true awareness knows how to impart that wisdom. He is aware of both the goal and the path. There has been a continuous lineage of such Self-realized souls occurring in this country since time immemorial.

In the *Mahābhārata*, Sage Vyāsa declares: "*Yadihāsti tadanyatra yēnnēhāsti na tat kvacit*" ("Whatever is found here (*Mahābhārata*) may be seen elsewhere, but what is not here will not be found anywhere else") (1.62.53). This verse, ostensibly about the tale of the *Mahābhārata* and of Bhāratam, has a deeper meaning. It points to the scope and structure of the human mind, the gamut of events in the *Mahābhārata* culminating in the battlefield of Kurukṣētra relating subtly to the drama that unfolds within. 'Bhāratam' is interpreted to mean the realm in which people revel in spiritual light; light is a metaphor often used to portray spiritual realities, a symbol common to all religions.

The *Mahābhārata* is a spectacular compendium of legends, moral stories, tales of personal conflicts, and learned disquisitions on ethics, law, philosophy, history, geography, genealogy and religion. It draws from a wide palette of human emotions such as love, hatred, deception, betrayal, letdowns and every other hue of human propensity, thus painting a variegated picture of the endless diversities and contradictions of the human mind. Kurukṣētra symbolizes the battleground within, the positive and negative energies clashing to gain supremacy. Conflict arises from imbalance and, more often, the disharmony that any one-sided attitude tends to perpetrate.

Dharma is the basis of peace and happiness. Whenever there is a preponderance of evil, the *Bhagavad Gītā* assures us of divine intervention. However, we often forget that the Lord's incarnation is not just physical; His birth augurs the dawn of truth within us. The *Gītā* is not only to be read; its salient teachings must be assimilated and absorbed.

The mind must expel vice in order to bring forth harmony. It is easy to delude and flatter ourselves by thinking we are good and those who oppose us are wicked. The greatest deceiver in the world is the mind. All unrighteousness springs from the six cardinal evils residing within. This siege will continue unless Kṛṣṇa is born in one's heart. Then, we can integrate mind and intellect, and thus attain the state of yōga.

Instead of blaming external factors, we must analyze and identify our own shortcomings, motivated by inner tendencies such as anger, greed and lust. We have all heard of the adage that when the forefinger is pointed in accusation of someone, three fingers point at oneself. It implies that the faults we find in another have their origin within. Understandably, this must be nature's way to make us look inward. So, instead of launching remedial measures to change external factors, we must take steps to refine the inner faculty. There should be no doubt that the easiest and most accessible entity is the 'I,' and this warrants a focusing on the Self.

The mind is generally regarded as a constituent of the human body, and confined within it. The irony is that it spans out to infinite limits transcending the body. So, the mind is pervasive, but being inanimate, it cannot shine by itself; unless the Self illumines it, the mind is inert. Just as a mirror layered with dust on its surface hinders clear reflection, the indulgent mind cannot engage in true introspection unless it sheds the sheaths of negativity, and relentlessly invokes the sublime consciousness, thus enriching and elevating itself.

Amma advises: "A meditative mind and spiritual understanding are necessary in order to attain clarity and subtlety in our thoughts and actions. The ordinary mind is like a pool of stagnant water. The stench issuing from it can cause discomfort to others. We ought to let this flow out and merge with the sea, and then the unpleasant smell is overcome. Likewise, our mind should be connected to the Divine, and then it will become as deep as the sea."

There is a story recounted by Swāmi Rāma Tīrtha about a Master's hermitage, where a number of disciples were staying to acquire spiritual knowledge. After completing their studies, the disciples wanted to return home with the Master's blessings. Knowing the minds of the disciples, the Guru asked, "Would you all like to go back home?" The disciples nodded. The Master then asked if the students thought they had learned everything that was to be learned, to which all but one said yes; the sole dissenter remained silent. When queried about his silence, he replied that he would like to go but thought that there was something of great importance that he had not learned yet. The Master gave the other students permission to leave, but asked the earnest one to remain.

This disciple continued staying even when a new group of students joined the hermitage. But at the end of the new term, he felt the same way, a state of incompleteness in his learning. When the others of this group dispersed, he was asked to stay. Thus he continued with the next batch, at the end of which the Master repeated the same question: "Do you know everything you need to know?" The student was silent, which prompted the preceptor to ask, "Do you want to go back?" This time the disciple smiled by way of an answer.

Having begun to perceive the entire world as part of himself, the question of 'going' or 'coming' was meaningless. He did not answer the question nor even acknowledge or prostrate before the Guru, and instead became deeply meditative. At this, the Master said, "You seem to have known what there is to know; there is nothing more you need to learn." Complimenting him on the focus with which he had continued his search for true knowledge, the Master designated him as the befitting guide for the students to come in the future, and entrusted him with the exclusive responsibility of teaching them. One should understand that all learning begins with the study of the Self, and ends in the realization that there is nothing more to be learned.

The *Chāndōgyōpaniṣad* reiterates, "*Yō vai bhūmā tat-sukham nālpē sukhamasti*" (7.23.1)—"Fullness is the source of all happiness that cannot be found in smaller entities."

43

Masterly Mandate

When Amma asked me to take charge of the āśram activities at Tiruvanantapuram after years of close tutelage under Her, I felt immense agony. The very idea of staying away from my beloved Amma was just unbearable. Whom would I turn to if I needed consolation? How would the days pass without hearing Amma's sweet voice, ambrosial words, and Her delectable laughter, and without seeing Her sunny smile? It was unthinkable, like being banished from paradise.

But at the same time, I knew that there was a definite purpose behind everything Amma says and does. A Guru always acts in the best interest of the disciple. By sending me away, Amma was adding to the training that She had already given me, so that I could withstand the storms and stresses of life. It is the hottest furnace that tempers the best steel.

In spite of all the logic I could muster, Amma's directive distressed me greatly, and the anguish expressed itself first as a few teardrops. Discerning the pain of Her grown-up child, Amma comforted me, saying, "*Karayāteṭā, Ammatan-*

neyallēṭā nī" ("Don't cry, my son. After all, you are Amma in every way!").

Helpless and limited as I am, I was aware that I could not be equated with Amma from my level, whereas in Her view, everyone was an extension of Herself, and so She perceived no difference. I am reminded of Socrates's advice, which stressed equanimity of mind: "Remember that there is nothing stable in human affairs; therefore, avoid undue elation in prosperity, or undue depression in adversity."

Amma then gave a discourse on the finer points of administration, which had all the characteristics of a lesson in human resource development (HRD). This sermon was, however, from the Master's curriculum of management. She emphatically said, "You may do a world of good to people, but do not get disillusioned when people criticize you for the smallest mistake and speak badly about you. Remember that this is the character of the world. However much you may help society, if you do it with the conviction that none will speak a good word about you in return, then, son, you will never ever be disappointed!"

Amma has said that even though we may do a hundred good things, the nature of the world is such that it disregards all the good we have done and waits for us to make one mistake. The Guru, in contrast, forbears all our mistakes, and waits patiently for us to do one good thing.

Pausing briefly, Amma continued, "Perform your duties without any specific intention of reforming others. Do it with an attitude that helps to enhance your own sense of self-satisfaction. Your attitude ought to be akin to an offering that is aimed at your spiritual elevation."

As is Her wont, Amma illustrated the import of Her words through an analogy. She said that a rose plant is fertilized and nourished with the manure of a mixture of used tea leaves and egg shells. The feed, though unattractive, causes the plants to bear healthy, beautiful and fragrant roses. Amma made Her point loud and clear, that I should not bother about the adversities that may play up in my role as administrator as long as the objective was to serve and deliver results as eye-catching and aromatic as the roses.

Amma's point is that the purpose of karma is to reform ourselves, not anybody else. In performing our actions with such an attitude, we can pave the way to Self-realization, which is greater than any worldly wealth. An instance in the *Mahābhārata* comes to mind, where after discoursing on supreme knowledge, Sage Vyāsa tells his son and disciple Śuka:

> *Yadyapyasya mahīm dadyād ratnapūrṇāmimām naraḥ*
> *Idamēva tataḥ śrēya iti manyēta tatvavit*
>
> Even if this earth, fully laden with gems, were to be offered to the wise man, he will think that much more

sublime is this (knowledge of the Self).

(Mahābhārata, 12.245.20)

What a beautiful and unique parental thought from the father himself, giving his son only the best advice for the noble path.

Jalal-al-Din Muhammad Rumi's line, "Your task is not to seek for love, but merely to seek and find all the barriers within yourself that you have built against it," further reveals the import of Amma's words to me that day.

44

Anchoritic Acuity

A scholar may win a debate by wielding his masterly knowledge of the subject and by the clever use of words, but it is not possible for anyone to substitute the pure experience of the Supreme with words, no matter how polished; That remains inaccessible to word or thought.

I am reminded of the following mantra from the *Taittirīyōpaniṣad*.

> *Yatō vācō nivartantē aprāpya manasā saha*
>
> (The realm) from where words with the mind return, unable to reach it. (2.4.1)

Silence is characteristic of wisdom. Those who doubt seek explanation. In the wake of experience, rationalization and elucidation cease. When doubts increase, one becomes verbose. Conversely, the more spiritual experience one has, the more silent he becomes. Once, Śrī Rāmakṛṣṇa told a person who was fond of engaging in lengthy debates, "If you wish to understand the matter in a single word, come here to me. If you wish to engage in a logical debate and analysis, then go to Kēśav."[50]

The claims of material scientists cannot be accepted as incontrovertible because later developments can prove them either inadequate or inaccurate or both. Meteorologists can forecast the weather for the near future, a few days at most, but beyond that, predictions are not foolproof. A phenomenon known as 'sensitive dependence on initial conditions,' sometimes referred to as the 'butterfly effect' (a butterfly flapping its wings in South America can affect the weather in Central Park in New York), vitiates the long-term predictability of the weather. Skewed perceptions of the truth as well as an overvaluation of rationale and logic prove inadequate in explaining many of life's great mysteries, leaving science tentative in its guesswork about nature.

Albert Einstein, who won the Nobel Prize for his singularly remarkable contributions to quantum physics, believed that only the deeper principles of truth could resolve uncertainties in science. He said, "One thing I have learned in my long life—that all our science measured against reality is primitive and childlike."

Whereas mathematicians admit that the concept of infinity is relative since they cannot conceptualize the ultimate

50 *A contemporary scholar.*

reality, the ancient sages in their inner wisdom introduced the concept of zero (*śūnyam*—0), a number that denotes completeness. The Cartesian axiom, 'I think, therefore I am,' ought to be reworded as 'I am, therefore I think,' to reflect the experience of the sages and ascetics who went to the root of the matter by contemplation. In truth, they are the real scientists. It has been said, "The intuitive mind is a sacred gift and the rational mind is a faithful servant. We have created a society that honors the servant and has forgotten the gift."

The limited human intellect cannot find perfect solutions to problems that threaten the well-being of society. If our questions pertain to gross matters, we can arrive at answers in the outside world. However, the more subtle the issue, the more one has to probe within. For example, to the question, "Who am I?" one has to seek the answer within. The ultimate answer, therefore, can only arise from awareness of the Self.

Physical sciences are incomplete since the issues can become divergent when the search for clarity leads to many other connected subjects, increasing the complications at each level, thus diffusing the one-pointed focus. Not only that, because importance is not given to the observer at any stage, the so-called objective sciences remain tinged by a subjective bias. In contrast, spirituality is essentially the study of the Self, i.e. the study of one's own being. The focus is solely on the subject, and is not diffused by other considerations. When the seeker eventually discovers his Self, he realizes his oneness with the whole of creation, since the Self in him is one with the Self pervading the whole universe. Thus his search attains fullness.

Generally, a meaningful study of any experience entails three factors: the experiencer, the experience itself, and the object of experience (experienced). The spiritual pursuit encompasses all three, unlike physical science, which is restricted only to the object of study, and is hence incomplete, not least because it is impossible to learn about everything in the manifold universe. The understanding that the universe is the mind itself inspires a bright and intelligent seeker to opt for the study of his own inner instrument (mind), which leads him to Self-realization. He then becomes aware of everything because the fact that creation at large is not separate or different from his own Self dawns on him. The experience is all-inclusive, conferring on the seeker of Truth fulfillment and everlasting bliss.

Indian philosophy in its entirety is rooted in the broad vision of seeing every part or element connected inherently to the whole, or as Kṛṣṇa said, "*Sūtrē maṇigaṇā iva*" (*Bhagavad Gītā*, 7.7.) ("Like the pearls held together on a thread").

It is said that Ampere, the renowned genius who discovered electrodynamics, would speak highly on the profundity of the subject. Talking to his friend Ozanam, he would say with bowed head, "How great is God, Ozanam; and how negligible is our science!"

In today's world, where small measures of scientific brilliance are hailed as sensational, and the individuals and organizations involved are eulogized, it is ironic that the universe, with its eternal mysteries and perplexing wonders that have eluded the rational understanding of the scientific community, is not rousing anyone to marvel and worship God—the super-intelligent creator, sustainer and destroyer of the cosmos.

When Amma says that we should try to practice meditation with open eyes, She is counseling us to perceive divinity in everything we see, whether sentient or insentient. By invoking the divine in everything we do, we can foster greater degrees of sensitivity to the myriad manifestations of godliness, paving the way to realization; thus karma becomes karma-yoga.

A king, desiring to celebrate his son's coronation in a grand fashion, asked his prime minister to organize festivities, stipulating that the best artists be brought in to perform during the event. When it came to selecting the best dancer for the event, the prime minister encountered a problem; a renowned dancer was the natural choice for the performance, but when the minister contacted her, she turned down the invitation, explaining that she had retired in order to pursue spiritual practices.

Afraid that he might lose his image or even his life if he failed to persuade her to perform for the coronation, the minister pleaded with her, explaining his predicament. Taking pity on the minister's dilemma, the danseuse agreed to perform on one condition: that a certain recluse be present among the audience.

The minister instantly agreed, started a countrywide search and, just before the event, managed to locate the person. At first, the recluse summarily rejected the request. Later, on learning more about the minister's predicament and feeling sorry for him, the hermit agreed to attend the performance that night. However, he insisted on one condition: that none should hold him back from leaving once the performance was over. Seeing no problem with this stipulation, the minister readily agreed.

The king and the royal family arrived, and the hermit was seated next to them. The show started with the gorgeous and graceful danseuse treating the audience to a superb display

of artistry, elegance and style. While the viewers were still engrossed in the show, the recluse suddenly stood up and walked out. The king, furious at the show of disrespect to the performer and the affront to the royal family, ordered his arrest.

When the recluse was brought to the king's presence, the monarch demanded, "How dare you walk out of the show when the performance was not over, and leave ahead of the king?"

The ascetic replied, "Firstly, I had insisted on the right to leave when the performance was over. Secondly, I got up and walked away only when the dancer had finished her performance."

"No, the dancer had not finished!" exploded the king.

At this, the recluse led the king to the stage and requested the thin white cloth spread on the stage where the danseuse had just finished performing to be removed. The white covering, with a thin layer of powder coated on its underside, was removed, revealing the impression of a beautiful, perfectly executed design of a 1,008-petaled lotus that the dancer had created with her feet. The king and the people around were amazed.

While the spectators had been absorbed in the dancer's physical attributes—her figure, dress and body movements—the recluse had been intently watching the subtle movements of her feet as they created the form of a lotus. As soon as the 1,008th petal had been created, and when the dancer had started winding up her performance, her reverse movement outlining the stem of the lotus, the hermit had stood up and walked away.

Such is the real scientist—one who can perceive the subtle aspects of things. In the recluse's astonishing awareness, we can find a clear instance of meditation with open eyes.

45

Sagely Subtlety

The mind can become either our greatest asset or our greatest liability on the pilgrimage to Truth. It can throw dust into our eyes and delude us. But when purified by karma yoga, the resulting awareness can lucidly reflect our flaws, thus helping us to rectify them. When the mind gains sufficient discrimination, it becomes an asset, guiding us towards our ultimate destiny. The battlefield of Kurukṣētra symbolizes the struggle between good and evil that continues to wage war within the human heart in its effort to find peace and happiness. The Pāṇḍavas and Kauravas represent the forces of good and evil respectively, preparing for a final showdown. In the mind's blind quest to annex material pleasures, it overlooks the option of being used as an instrument of the Divine, and often drifts away from the rightful path and onto the path of *adharma* (unrighteousness).

Peace and joy prevailed in ancient Bhāratam, regardless of differences in standards of affluence, because people followed the path of dharma. The extent to which one adheres to dharma is directly proportionate to an individual's sense of well-being.

Often, the Guru asks us to focus the mind by looking inward. We close our eyes and struggle to direct our gaze within. (It may be necessary for a beginner to close his eyes to avoid external distractions.) Incapable of seeing even any of the organs inside our own body with our naked eyes, we continue to look within, this endeavor based on the assumption that the mind is something within our body. In truth, the mind is nothing other than the idea that 'I am the body' or this sense of 'I-ness.' It pervades 'inside' and 'outside' alike, transcends the physical body, and identifies with the created world at large. So, when the Guru tells us to look within, He does not mean anything literal. 'Looking within' is nothing but observing ourselves, i.e. watching all the activities of the mind, both when the eyes are closed and when they are open. It is the Jīvātma that provides power to the inanimate mind. In actual fact, the act of turning our focus inside implies the need to withdraw the senses from their attachment to objects of the external world and to direct them to the luminescence of the soul; hence the relevance of closing the eyes. When the mind with all the power at its command tries to foil these efforts, we have to use *vivēka* (discrimination, i.e. differentiating between the eternal and ephemeral) to subdue it in order to delve deeper into the Self.

There is a story about a woodcutter who made a living by cutting trees from a nearby forest and selling the firewood. Everyday, he would pass a sage engrossed in meditation. Once, he approached the monk and sought his blessings, only to be told by the sage "to go deep inside." Taking the direction literally, he went deeper into the woods, and to his surprise found a number of sandalwood trees, which he cut and made good money. However, after a few days, recalling the advice of the sage, he went deeper into the forest and discovered a silver mine, a great prospect for enriching him all the more. When he went to thank the sage, the latter told him to go even deeper into the woods. Going into the inner recesses of the jungle, overcoming formidable obstacles in the threatening environment, he sighted a gold mine, but an inner voice told him to go even deeper into the forest. Disregarding the adversities he faced, he kept moving. Some time later, he was stunned to find a diamond mine.

Notwithstanding the possibility of becoming immensely wealthy, his recent discoveries set him thinking. Only a few weeks earlier, he had been a very poor man, and now, here was a cache of diamond and other gems that could make him unimaginably rich. But the thought of the sage, who despite the knowledge of the riches seemed very happy sitting in meditation, kept haunting him! Realizing the subtle import of the sage's words, the woodcutter went back to him to seek the latter's blessings once again. The sage received him and told him to look into the heart and continue to move deeper and deeper until he found his real Self.

Looking and inquiring within ever more deeply is spirituality; delving into the outer world is worldliness. The nature of worldly desires is such that they multiply and eventually overwhelm us, the dwindling self-control culminating in self-destruction. In contrast, desire for emancipation takes one ultimately to a state of desirelessness, wherein one finds utmost fulfillment. The real science is the science of the Self. This is referred to as 'Śāstra.'

Emphasizing the need for regular sādhanā, Amma says, "Continuous practice helps a beginner rein in his mind. Just as merely sweeping a room can remove only the superficial dirt whereas using a wet mop can also release the grime sticking to the floor, constant sādhanā can subdue the instinctive longings of the mind."

She drives home the necessity of spiritual practice with a few analogies. "The experienced climber does not need a ladder to climb a tree whereas the beginner does. Birds in the air do not need to follow traffic rules but motorists and pedestrians on the ground have to follow them for their own safety."

Until we reach the goal, every spiritual aspirant needs both a path to the ultimate as well as an authentic guide who can take him there. One who is established in the Supreme never repudiates the importance of either the path or the guide.

It is often said that science is progressing, but in spite of all its undeniable contributions, problems continue to perplex the world. Despite all the scientific advances made over the years and centuries, we continue to live in fear, uncertainty and insecurity. Why is the essential element, 'piece of mind,' ever eluding us? There is more instability, strife and unhappiness, if anything, than ever before. This is not surprising since material science does not encompass the knowledge of true living or the values underlying a harmonious life.

Śrī Kṛṣṇa is unequivocal in His advice to Arjuna in the *Bhagavad Gītā*:

> *Tasmācchāstram pramāṇam tē kāryākāryavyavasthitau*
> *jñatvā śāstravidhānōktam karma kartumihārhasi*
>
> O Arjuna! The śāstra (scripture) is your authority in deciding what you should or should not do. You are to act according to scriptural injunctions here in this world. (16.24)

Material wealth is never the only factor determining happiness, which is a state of mind. However, steady corruption in lifestyles over the last few decades has led to a marked indifference to, bordering on total disregard of, the old traditions, undermining peace of mind and satisfaction. Even though the quality of physical comforts has increased markedly, these comforts have failed to increase mental peace and security.

If value-based customs and practices had been retained along with progresses in science and technology, we would be enjoying much more happiness and contentment today. In Her discourses, Amma speaks in simple terms about the principle of happiness, reiterating that it lies in the mind and not in the object of immediate pleasure. She gives the example of being tempted to consume many '*laḍḍūs*' (a confectionery) when offered a plateful. We might relish the first laḍḍū immensely. The second one may not give us the same amount of pleasure as the first, and with the third and fourth, diminishing returns set in, eventually culminating in stomach ache. However, the vāsanā (latent tendency) for eating laḍḍūs is actually strengthened.

By the same logic, the more we habituate ourselves to spiritual contemplation, the more our vāsanā for spiritual pursuits will be reinforced, but unlike outer objects, the law of diminishing returns will not set in; in contrast, the enjoyment of the inner depths of the soul increases, until we become sweetness itself.

Bhartṛhari's verse from *Vairāgyaśatakam* illumines the understanding:

Bhōgā na bhuktā vayamēva bhuktā-
Stapō na taptam vayamēva taptāḥ
Kālō na yātō vayamēva yātā-
Stṛṣṇā na jīrṇā vayamēva jīrṇāḥ

We did not enjoy the pleasures of the world but were being enjoyed by them. Instead of undergoing the heat of penance, we underwent the heat of worldly sorrows. It is not time that has passed, but that we have wasted time. It is not desires that have been exhausted but we. (7)

In the *Mahābhārata*, one of the stories Bhīṣma tells Yudhiṣṭhira to illustrate the blessedness of a human birth is about a learned person, poor by birth, who was knocked down by a speeding chariot ridden by an affluent and wicked local merchant. The man sustained serious injuries in the accident and became distressed, thinking that this had happened to him only because he was poor. He began to feel bad about his lot, and decided that without sufficient wealth, life was meaningless and wretched. He decided to commit suicide.

As the scholar was preparing to end his life, his plight caught the attention of Indra, the chief of the *dēvas* (gods), who felt sorry for him and decided to help. He assumed the form of a jackal and appeared before the man. Seeing him making preparations for self-immolation, Indra asked him why he was taking that extreme step. The poor man explained the reasons for his decision, emphasizing the worthlessness of a life bedeviled by poverty, which appeared to attract only rejection and lack of recognition from society.

The celestial lord pacified him, saying that a human life was far superior to all others in the first place, and that to be learned and accomplished in traditional knowledge was a bonus that elevated life to the highest pedestal. Reminding him that he was blessed with both attributes, Indra said that it was sheer foolishness to give up his life in disillusionment. He pointed out that a human birth was far superior to that of an animal, although false pride led man to misery and eventual downfall. "My earnest advice to you is to rid yourself of this false pride and return home. This human birth is neither to be frittered away nor destroyed. Your affluence lies in the fact that you are born human and are learned. Do not think of ending this valuable life. Go home!" Saying so, Indra disappeared.

As two soldiers lay reminiscing under the starlit sky in a remote field camp, the first one asked, "What made you join the army?"

The other replied, "I had no wife and loved war, and so ended up here. How about you?"

The first one said, "I had a wife and loved peace, and so I came here!"

Life is replete with such baffling paradoxes. In answer to a question of a devotee, Amma had this to say, "Human beings have two major problems. One of them arises when you do not get what you desire. The other problem is strange because it arises when you get what you desire." In brief, our happiness should not depend on the objects of the world.

Clarifying the doubt of the questioner further, Amma said, "Attachment makes us cling to what we have acquired. This increases our possessive tendencies. As a result, the mind becomes restless, whether or not we have obtained what we want. The struggle to safeguard whatever had been gained results in the loss of peace of mind."

A mahātma never claims anything as his own. For him, there is no sense of duality, and hence he has nothing to lose. Only if another alternative existed would there be a loss. Is there anything in the material world that we can claim as our own? Isn't it necessary to cast away even the body in the morrows we consider ours?

There is a popular saying, "The pessimist complains about the wind; the optimist expects it to change; the realist

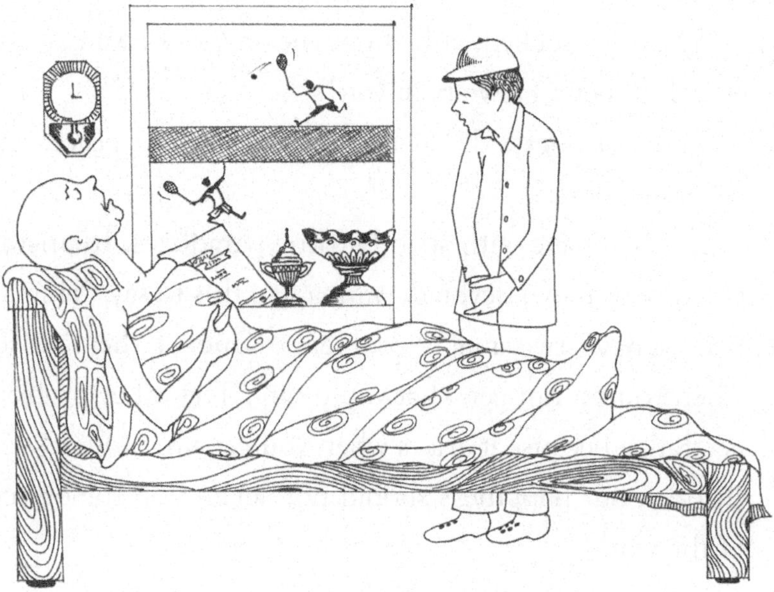

adjusts the sails." Life becomes worthwhile only if it is taken in its true spirit and lived from moment to moment.

Among the fan mail that Arthur Ashe, the legendary tennis player, received when he was terminally ill with AIDS, one was profoundly sentimental. It asked, "Why does God have to select you for such a bad disease?"

Arthur Ashe's reply remains an inspiration to the despondent and suffering everywhere: "The world over, 50 million children start playing tennis, 5 million learn to play tennis, 500,000 learn professional tennis, 50,000 come to the circuit, 5,000 reach the Grand Slam, 50 reach Wimbledon, four to the semi-finals, and two to the finals. When I was holding a cup, I never asked God, 'Why me?' And today, in pain, I should not be asking God, 'Why me?'"

In a way, the best friend to all beings is Death, simply because it stays with us all the time.

Focusing on the objective of life, Kabīr, an Indian saint and poet, sang:

Kabīr sūtā kyā karē kūṭhē kāj nivār
jis panthu tū cālnā sōī panth samvār

Arise from slumber, O Kabīr, divest yourself of the rubbish. Be focused and take the path you were meant to tread.

Standing under the unbounded canopy of the inky night sky, the roar of the rising ocean waves enhancing the quiet sanctity of this cozy peninsula, I was nostalgically reminiscing about the events leading to my providential meeting of Amma and the magical days that followed. As I began to reflect on the stroke of good luck that had brought me to this sacred abode, I wondered if it was just coincidence, or if my arrival here had been predetermined. The following verse comes to mind:

Yōnimanyē prapadyantē śarīratvāya dēhinaḥ
Sthāṇumanyēऽnusamyanti yathā karma yathā śrutam

> Some souls enter wombs to assume new bodies while others become non-moving forms in keeping with their actions and knowledge (acquired from previous births).
>
> *(Kaṭhōpaniṣad, 2.2.7)*

Singularly rare is the opportunity to meet someone like Amma *and* to come under Her scintillating guidance. She is a Mother, who dispenses manna for our nourishment, and a Master whose mandate will, if honored, lead us to mōkṣa.

Will we have the same opportunities in forthcoming births as we do now with Amma? Who knows? What matters is how we approach Amma and how we receive Her *now.*

We are in possession of a rare gift, the human body. It is *dharma sādhanam*, a precious instrument for upholding dharma. The body is not meant for accentuating body consciousness; it is to be utilized to promote Self-awareness.

Amma's *raison d'etre* is the reinstatement of dharma, and thus, by adhering to Her teachings, we can reach the spiritual horizon of Truth. The Sun of Spirituality shines before us as the Divine Mother and Master, Amma. Let us pray with wide-open hearts for Amma's grace and blessings. *Aum amṛtēśwaryai namaḥ!*

Glossary

Acchan—Malayāḷam word for 'father.'

Ādi Śankarācārya—Saint who is believed to have lived between the eighth and ninth centuries AD, and who is revered as a Guru and chief proponent of the *Advaita* (non-dual) philosophy.

Adharma—Unrighteousness. Deviation from natural harmony.

Advaita—Not two; non-dual; philosophy that holds that the *jīva* (individual soul) and *jagat* (universe) are ultimately one with *Brahman*, the Supreme Reality.

Amma(chi)—Malayāḷam word for 'mother.'

Amṛtapuri—International headquarters of the Mātā Amṛtānandamayī Maṭh, located at Amma's birth place in Kēraḷa, India.

Ārati—Clockwise movement of a lamp aflame with burning camphor, to propitiate a deity, usually signifying the closing of a ceremonial worship.

Āśram—Monastery. Amma defines it as a compound: '*ā*'—'that' and '*śramam*'—'effort' (toward Self-realization).

Ātma—Self or Soul.

Aum/Ōm—Primordial sound in the universe; the seed of creation; the cosmic sound, which can be heard in deep meditation; the Holy Word, taught in the Upaniṣads, which signifies *Brahman*, the divine ground of existence.

Aum Amṛtēśwaryai Namaḥ—"Salutations to the Goddess of Immortality (Amma)."

Aum Namaḥ Śivāya—"I bow down to the Eternally Auspicious One."

Avadhūtā—An enlightened person whose behavior transcends social norms.

Bhagavad Gītā—Literally, 'Song of the Lord,' it consists of 18 chapters of verses in which Lord Kṛṣṇa advises Arjuna. The advice is given on the battlefield of Kurukṣētra, just before the righteous Pāṇḍavas fight the unrighteous Kauravas. It is a practical guide to overcoming crises in one's personal or social life, and is the essence of Vēdic wisdom.

Bhagawān—The Lord; "*Bhagam yasyāsti saḥ Bhagawān,*" i.e. Bhagawān is one who is endowed with the six attributes called '*bhagam.*' According to *Viṣṇu Purāṇam*, "*Aiśvaryasya samagrasya vīryasya yaś-asaḥ śriyaḥ jñānavairāgyayōścaiva ṣaṇṇām bhaga itīritāḥ*"—Bhagam comprises supremacy, valor, fame, prosperity, knowledge and dispassion.

Bhajan—Devotional song or hymn in praise of God

Bhakti—Devotion for the Lord.

Bhāratam—The realm in which people revel in spiritual light; another word for India.

Bhāva—Divine mood.

Bhaya-bhakti—Devotion inspired by fear of repercussion.

Brahmā—Lord of Creation in the Hindu Trinity.

Brahman—Ultimate Truth beyond any attributes; the Supreme Reality underlying all life; the divine ground of existence.

Brahmacāri—Celibate male disciple who practices spiritual disciplines under a Guru's guidance. ('*Brahmacāriṇi*' is the female equivalent.)

Brāhmin—One who belongs to the priestly caste. The four main castes in Indian society are *Brāhmaṇa* (priestly clan), *Kṣatriya* (martial clan), *Vaiśya* (trading community) and *Śūdra* (serving community).

Buddha—From '*budh*' (to know, to wake up); a reference to Sage Gautama Buddha.

Darśan—Audience with a holy person or a vision of the Divine.

Dēvas—Celestial beings.

Dēvī—Goddess/Divine Mother.

Dēvī Bhāva—'The Divine Mood of Dēvī,' the state in which Amma reveals Her oneness and identity with the Divine Mother.

Dharma—Literally, 'that which upholds (creation).' Generally used to refer to the harmony of the universe, a righteous code of conduct, sacred duty or eternal law.

Durgā—One of the forms of the Goddess.

Dwāpara—See '*yuga*.'

Gō*pa*—Cowherd boy from Vṛndāvan.

Gō*pī*—Milk maiden from Vṛndāvan. The gōpīs were known for their ardent devotion to Lord Kṛṣṇa. Their devotion exemplifies the most intense love for God.

Guru—Spiritual teacher.

G*urukula*— Literally, the clan (*kula*) of the preceptor (G*uru*); traditional school where students would stay with the Guru for the entire duration of their scriptural studies.

Iṣṭa dēvata—Preferred form of divinity.

Japa—Repeated chanting of a *mantra.*

Jīvātma—Individual Self or Soul.

Jñāna—Knowledge of the Truth.

Jñānamudrā—The mystic gesture of knowledge: the index finger is bent so that its tip is joined with the tip of the thumb, with the other three fingers spread out.

Kaḷari—Generally, a center for martial arts training; here, it refers to a temple where Amma used to hold Kṛṣṇa Bhāva and Dēvī Bhāva darśans.

Karma—Action; mental, verbal and physical activity.

Karma Yōga—The way of action, the path of selfless service.

Kauravas—The 101 children of King Dhṛtarāṣtra and Queen Gāndhāri, of whom the unrighteous Duryōdhana was the eldest. The Kauravas were the enemies of their cousins, the virtuous Pāṇḍavas, with whom they fought in the Mahābhārata War.

Kṛṣṇa—From '*kṛṣ,*' meaning 'to draw to oneself' or 'to remove sin;' principal incarnation of Lord Viṣṇu.

He was born into a royal family but was raised by foster parents, and lived as a cowherd boy in Vṛndāvan, where He was loved and worshipped by His devoted companions, the gōpīs and gōpas. Kṛṣṇa later established the city of Dwāraka. He was a friend and advisor to His cousins, the Pāṇḍavas, especially Arjuna, whom He served as charioteer during the Mahābhārata War, and to whom He revealed His teachings as the *Bhagavad Gītā*.

Kṛṣṇa Bhāva—'The Divine Mood of Kṛṣṇa,' the state in which Amma reveals Her oneness and identity with Lord Kṛṣṇa.

Kuññu—'Little One.' Some devotees used to call Amma '*Kuññu*' or '*Ammachi-kuññu*.' '*Kuññē*' is the vocative form.

Lakṣmaṇa—Younger brother of Rāma.

Līlā—Divine play.

Mahātma—Literally, 'great soul.' Used to describe those who have attained spiritual realization.

Malayāḷam—Language spoken in the Indian state of Kēraḷa.

Mangaḷasūtra / Māngalyasūtra—See '*tāli*.'

Mantra—A sound, syllable, word or words of spiritual

content. According to Vēdic commentators, mantras are revelations of ṛṣis arising from deep contemplation.

Mantra dīkṣa—Initiation by mantra, sometimes involving rituals.

Manu—Progenitor of humanity.

Maṭh—Hindu monastery.

Māyā—Cosmic delusion, personified as a temptress. Illusion; appearance, as contrasted with Reality; the creative power of the Lord.

Mīnākṣī—Literally, one whose eyes are in fish-shaped; a form of the Goddess. This form is enshrined in a temple in Madurai; hence the sobriquet Madurai Mīnākṣī.

Mōkṣa—Spiritual liberation.

Mōḷ—'Daughter' in Malayāḷam.

Mōn—'Son' in Malayāḷam.

Mudrā—Gesture formed by the hands and fingers, and having a mystical import.

Narasimha—Half-lion, half-human incarnation of Viṣṇu.

Nṛtta—Dance.

Pāṇḍavas—Five sons of King Pāṇḍu, and cousins of Kṛṣṇa.

Paramātma—Supreme Self.

Pārvatī—Consort of Lord Śiva.

Pāyasam—Sweet pudding.

Pīṭham—Low platform; seat for the Guru.

Praṇava—The mystic syllable 'Aum.'

Prāṇa—Vital force.

Prajāpati—God presiding over creation; an epithet of Brahmā, the Creator; any one of the 10 *ṛṣis* created by Brahmā at the beginning of the creation.

Prasād(am)—Blessed offering or gift from a holy person or temple, often in the form of food.

Pūja—Ritualistic or ceremonial worship.

Puruṣa—'Man' in Malayāḷam; 'Supreme Self' in Sānskṛt.

Purāṇas—Compendium of stories—including the biographies and stories of gods, saints, kings and great people—allegories and chronicles of great historical events that aim to make the teachings of the Vēdas simple and available to all.

Putracchan—The local appellation for the Buddha in Māvēlikkara.

Rāma—The divine hero of the epic *Rāmāyaṇa.* An incarnation of Lord Viṣṇu, he is considered the ideal man of dharma and virtue. '*Ram*' means 'to revel;' one who revels in himself; the principle of joy within; also one who gladdens the hearts of others.

Ramaṇa Maharṣi—Enlightened spiritual master (1879 - 1950) who lived in Tiruvaṇṇāmalai in Tamiḷ Nāḍu. He recommended Self-inquiry as the path to Liberation, though he approved a variety of paths and spiritual practices.

Ṛṣi—Seers to whom mantras were revealed in deep meditation.

Sādhanā—Spiritual practice. Also a body of disciplines, a way of life, which leads to the supreme goal of Self-realization.

Sādhak—Spiritual aspirant or seeker.

Sahasranāma—Thousand names.

Samādhi—Literally, 'cessation of all mental movements;' oneness with God; a transcendental state in which one loses all sense of individual identity; union with Absolute Reality; a state of intense concentration in which consciousness is completely unified.

Samsāra—Cycle of births and deaths; the world of flux; the wheel of birth, decay, death and rebirth.

Sankalpa—Divine resolve, usually used in association with mahātmas.

Sanātana Dharma—Literally, 'Eternal Religion' or 'The Eternal Way of Life,' the original and traditional name for Hinduism.

Sanyāsi—A monk who has taken formal vows of renunciation (*sanyāsa*); traditionally wears an ocher-colored robe, representing the burning away of all desires. The female equivalent is a *sanyāsini.*

Śāstra—Science; in the context of this book, authoritative scriptural texts.

Sēva—Selfless service, the results of which are dedicated to God.

Śiva—Worshipped as the first and the foremost in the lineage of Gurus, and as the formless substratum of the universe in relationship to Śakti. He is the Lord of destruction in the trinity of Brahmā (Lord of Creation), Viṣṇu (Lord of Sustenance), and Mahēśvara (Śiva).

Sītā—Rāma's holy consort. In India, She is considered to be the ideal of womanhood.

Śrī—A title of respect originally meaning 'divine,' 'holy' or 'auspicious;' now in modern India, simply a respectful form of address similar to 'Mr.'

Śrī Laḷitā Sahasranāma—Litany of 1,000 names of Śrī Laḷitā Dēvī, the Supreme Goddess.

Śrī Mātā Amṛtānandamayī Dēvī—Amma's official monastic name, meaning Mother of Immortal Bliss.

Śrī Rāmakṛṣṇa Paramahamsa—A 19th century spiritual Master from West Bengal, hailed as the apostle of religious harmony. He generated a spiritual renaissance that continues to touch the lives of millions.

Tāli—Necklace or pendant that the bridegroom ties around the bride's neck during the marriage rites; also known as '*mangaḷasūtra*' or '*māngalyasūtra*.'

Tapas—Austerities, penance.

Taravāṭ—The household of the main family in a matriarchal system.

Upaniṣad—The portions of the Vēdas dealing with Self-knowledge.

Vaḷḷikkāvu—Village across the river from the peninsula where the Amṛtapuri Āśram is located. Amma is sometimes referred to as 'Vaḷḷikkāvu Amma.'

Vāsanā—Latent tendencies or subtle desires within the mind that manifest as thought and action.

Vēdānta—'The end of the Vēdas.' It refers to the Upaniṣads, which deal with the subject of Brahman, the Supreme Truth, and the path to realize that Truth.

Vēdas—Most ancient of all scriptures, originating from God, the Vēdas were not composed by any human author but were 'revealed' in deep meditation to the ancient ṛṣis. These sagely revelations came to be known as Vēdas, of which there are four: *Ṛg*, *Yajus*, *Sāma* and *Atharva*.

Vēdic—Of or pertaining to the ancient Vēdas.

Vivēka—Discrimination, especially between the ephemeral and eternal.

Viṣṇu—Lord of Sustenance in the Hindu Trinity.

Yōga—"To unite." Union with the Supreme Being. A broad term, it also refers to the various methods of practices through which one can attain oneness with the Divine. A path that leads to Self-realization.

Yuga—According to Hindu cosmogony, the universe (from origin to dissolution) passes through a cycle made up of four Yugas or ages. The first is *Kṛta Yuga*, during which dharma reigns in society. Each succeeding age sees the progressive decline of dharma. The second age is known as *Trētā Yuga*, the third is *Dwāpara Yuga*, and the fourth and present epoch is known as *Kali Yuga*.

Acknowledgements

Reminiscing about Amma may be possible, especially when one has been blessed to be in Her order since its inception. However, I make no claims to presenting an intimate view of those events. Indeed, any such attempt at evoking those memories is tantamount to holding a candle to the sun.

This book demanded much support in terms of compilation and proof-reading, an integral part of any work. For these, I thank Menonji (Narayan Menon) for rendering all necessary help to make this effort fruitful. The typesetting, transliteration of Sānskṛt and vernacular verses, and the organization of the text were critical tasks that demanded extreme diligence. I am grateful to Udayan, who spared no pains in assisting me in these functions.

Effort has been made to enhance the text by a number of illustrations, including computer graphics, and this was possible only because of a few youngsters, whose spirit of application had been stupendous. I am indeed grateful to them for their contribution. Last but not least, I thank Satish, Ramachandran and Achuthan for their invaluable assistance and support during the preparation of the work.

I would like to close this section with a tribute to all the sanyāsis and sanyāsinis of Amma's order, and my other monastic colleagues and ashram residents. They have been part of my blissful journey along this path over the years. My reverential salutations also to nature—the flora and fauna—which are not only part of the beloved landscape but teachers in their own right, imparting lessons in self-sacrifice and renunciation. Like the deep sea and vast sky, they have remained blissful witnesses to the unconditional love and compassion Amma has proffered to humanity.

Pronunciation Guide

Vowels can be short or long:

a – as ‘u’ in but

ā – as ‘a’ in far

e – as e in pen

ē – as ‘a’ in name

i – as ‘i’ in pin

ī – as ‘ee’ in meet

o – as in pot

ō – as ‘o’ in mole

u – as ‘u’ in push

ū – as ‘oo’ in hoot

ṛ – as ri in rim

ḥ – pronounce ‘aḥ’ like ‘aha,’ ‘iḥ’ like ‘ihi,’ and ‘uḥ’ like ‘uhu.’

Most consonants are aspirated (e.g. kh) or not (e.g. k). The aspiration is part of the consonant. The examples given below are therefore only approximate.

k – as ‘k’ in ‘kite’

kh – as ‘ckh’ in ‘Eckhart’

g – as ‘g’ in ‘give’

gh – as 'g-h' in 'dig-hard'

c – as 'c' in 'cello'

ch – as 'ch-h' in 'staunch-heart'

j – as 'j' in 'joy'

jh – as 'dgeh' in 'hedgehog'

ñ – as 'ny' in 'canyon'

The letters d, t, n with dots under them are pronounced with the tip of the tongue against the roof of the mouth, the others with the tip against the teeth.

ṭ – as 't' in 'tub'

ṭh – as 'th' in 'lighthouse'

ḍ – as 'd' in 'dove'

ḍh – as 'dh' in 'red-hot'

ṇ – as 'n' in 'naught'

p – as 'p' in 'pine'

ph – as 'ph' in 'up-hill'

b – as 'b' in 'bird'

bh – as 'bh' in 'rub-hard'

m – as 'm' in 'mother'

y – as 'y' in 'yes'

r – as 'r' in Italian 'Roma' (rolled)

ḷ – as 'l' in 'like'

v – as w in when

ṣ – as 'sh' in 'shine'

ś – as 's' in German 'sprechen'
s – as 's' in 'sun'
h – as 'h' in 'hot'
With double consonants the initial sound only is pronounced twice:
cc – as 'tc' in 'hot chip'
jj – as 'dj' in 'red jet'

The 'ऽ' sign has been used when the vowel 'a' has been elided. For example, the word '*śivo*ऽ*ham*' is a compound of '*śivaḥ*' and 'aham.' When these words are conjoined, the initial vowel in 'aham' is elided, and the elision is indicated by the 'ऽ' sign.

Book Catalog

By Author

Sri Mata Amritanandamayi Devi

108 Quotes On Faith
108 Quotes On Love
Compassion, The Only Way To Peace: Paris Speech
Cultivating Strength And Vitality
Living In Harmony
May Peace And Happiness Prevail: Barcelona Speech
May Your Hearts Blossom: Chicago Speech
Practice Spiritual Values And Save The World: Delhi Speech
The Awakening Of Universal Motherhood: Geneva Speech
The Eternal Truth
The Infinite Potential Of Women: Jaipur Speech
Understanding And Collaboration Between Religions
Unity Is Peace: Interfaith Speech

Swami Amritaswarupananda Puri

Ammachi: A Biography
Awaken Children, Volumes 1-9
From Amma's Heart
Mother Of Sweet Bliss
The Color Of Rainbow

Swami Jnanamritananda Puri

Eternal Wisdom, Volumes 1-2

Swami Paramatmananda Puri

Dust Of Her Feet
On The Road To Freedom Volumes 1-2
Talks, Volumes 1-6

Swami Purnamritananda Puri

Unforgettable Memories

Swami Ramakrishnananda Puri

Eye Of Wisdom
Racing Along The Razor's Edge
Secret Of Inner Peace
The Blessed Life
The Timeless Path
Ultimate Success

Swamini Krishnamrita Prana

Love Is The Answer
Sacred Journey
The Fragrance Of Pure Love
Torrential Love

M.A. Center Publications

1,000 Names Commentary
Archana Book (Large)
Archana Book (Small)
Being With Amma
Bhagavad Gita
Bhajanamritam, Volumes 1-6
Embracing The World
For My Children
Immortal Light
Lead Us To Purity
Lead Us To The Light
Man And Nature
My First Darshan
Puja: The Process Of Ritualistic Worship
Sri Lalitha Trishati Stotram

Amma's Websites

AMRITAPURI—Amma's Home Page
Teachings, Activities, Ashram Life, eServices, Yatra, Blogs and News
http://www.amritapuri.org

AMMA (Mata Amritanandamayi)
About Amma, Meeting Amma, Global Charities, Groups and Activities and Teachings
http://www.amma.org

EMBRACING THE WORLD®
Basic Needs, Emergencies, Environment, Research and News
http://www.embracingtheworld.org

AMRITA UNIVERSITY
About, Admissions, Campuses, Academics, Research, Global and News
http://www.amrita.edu

THE AMMA SHOP—Embracing the World® Books & Gifts Shop
Blog, Books, Complete Body, Home & Gifts, Jewelry, Music and Worship
http://www.theammashop.org

IAM—Integrated Amrita Meditation Technique®
Meditation Taught Free of Charge to the Public, Students, Prisoners and Military
http://www.amma.org/groups/north-america/projects/iam-meditation-classes

AMRITA PUJA
Types and Benefits of Pujas, Brahmasthanam Temple, Astrology Readings, Ordering Pujas
http://www.amritapuja.org

GREENFRIENDS
Growing Plants, Building Sustainable Environments, Education and Community Building
http://www.amma.org/groups/north-america/projects/green-friends

FACEBOOK
This is the Official Facebook Page to Connect with Amma
https://www.facebook.com/MataAmritanandamayi

DONATION PAGE
Please Help Support Amma's Charities Here:
http://www.amma.org/donations

CPSIA information can be obtained
at www.ICGtesting.com
Printed in the USA
LVOW04s0509240516
489556LV00004B/5/P

9 781680 372847